Praise for
Janet Cheatham Bell
and her
Inspirational collections:

"I want to congratulate Janet Cheatham Bell on her insight and sensitivity.... *[Famous Black Quotations]* is an excellent and much-needed addition to the literature."

—EARL G. GRAVES, publisher, *Black Enterprise*

"Herein is the wisdom of a lifetime...."

—MARK VICTOR HANSEN,
co-creator of the *New York Times* bestselling
Chicken Soup for the Soul series

"Janet Cheatham Bell knows the power of words.... In her own inimitable way, she continues to shape our lives."

—DENNIS KIMBRO, Ph.D., director,
Clark Atlanta University Center for Entrepreneurship;
author of *Think and Grow Rich: A Black Choice*

TILL
VICTORY
IS
WON

FAMOUS BLACK
QUOTATIONS FROM
THE NAACP

EDITED BY

JANET CHEATHAM BELL

WASHINGTON SQUARE PRESS
PUBLISHED BY POCKET BOOKS
New York   London   Toronto   Sydney   Singapore

A WASHINGTON SQUARE PRESS *Original* publication

WSP A Washington Square Press Publication of
POCKET BOOKS, a division of Simon & Schuster, Inc.
1230 Avenue of the Americas, New York, NY 10020

ISBN 978-0-7434-2825-5

First Washington Square Press trade paperback printing February 2002

10 9 8 7 6 5 4 3 2 1

WASHINGTON SQUARE PRESS and colophon are registered trademarks of Simon & Schuster, Inc.

For information regarding special discounts for bulk purchases, please contact Simon & Schuster Special Sales at 1-800-456-6798 or business@simonandschuster.com

Printed in the U.S.A.

ACKNOWLEDGMENTS

The assistance and support of several people were essential or this book wouldn't be—Darcy Prather, who gave me the idea; Julian Bond, who patiently fielded my many questions and requests for help; Carole Hall, whose vision has made numerous resources available; my agent, Caroline Carney, who not only found a publisher, but goaded me to reveal my light; and my dedicated and astute editor, Tracy Sherrod. I am also grateful to Cleetta Ryals and the Reverend Floyd Davis, past president of the Chicago branch of the NAACP, whose early encouragement was important to my going forward with this project. Most of all, thanks to my son, Kamau, who provided a retreat and unconditional love when I really needed it.

My other friends and family, both old and new, who continue to believe in and encourage me, no matter what happens, are Claudia Allen, A'Lelia Bundles, Kevin Cheatham, Reginald Cheatham, Alvin Foster, Lillian Fleming, Lucille Freeman, Ellen Gary, Mary Ophelia Johnson, Dwayne Kennedy, Mary Anna Major, Miguel and Renee Mickey, Lottie Moore, Earnestine Nelson, Donn Nettles, Bill Pittman, Patricia Russell-McCloud, Madeline Scales-Taylor, Jason Smith, Marcella Taylor, Madganna and Bernard Wilson. My thanks to all of you for your kindness, love, and faith.

A strong and effective NAACP is as critical for white coexistence as it is for black progress.

KWEISI MFUME,
president and CEO of the NAACP since 1996

—•—

What happens to the NAACP is too important for African-Americans to sit on the sidelines taking potshots while waiting to see what happens.

MARY FRANCES BERRY,
chair, U.S. Commission on Civil Rights

CONTENTS

"Lift Every Voice and Sing"

Lift every voice and sing
Till earth and heaven ring,
Ring with the harmonies of Liberty;
Let our rejoicing rise
High as the listening skies,
Let it resound loud as the rolling sea.
Sing a song full of the faith that the dark past has taught us,
Sing a song full of the hope that the present has brought us,
Facing the rising sun of our new day begun
Let us march on till victory is won.

Stony the road we trod,
Bitter the chastening rod,
Felt in the days when hope unborn had died;
Yet with a steady beat,
Have not our weary feet
Come to the place for which our fathers sighed?
We have come over a way that with tears have been watered,
We have come, treading our path through the blood of the
    slaughtered,
Out from the gloomy past,
Till now we stand at last
Where the white gleam of our bright star is cast.

God of our weary years,
God of our silent tears,

Thou who has brought us thus far on the way;
Thou who has by Thy might
Led us into the light,
Keep us forever in the path, we pray.
Lest our feet stray from the places, our God, where we met
  Thee;
Lest, our hearts drunk with the wine of the world, we forget
  Thee;
Shadowed beneath Thy hand,
May we forever stand.
True to our God,
True to our native land.

"Lift Every Voice and Sing" by James Weldon Johnson.
By permission of the Estate of Grace and James Weldon Johnson.

FOREWORD

Quotations are useful in a variety of ways.

They can be read for education and inspiration.

They can add weight and heft to otherwise uninspired writing.

And they can powerfully or poignantly say for the speaker or writer what he or she might not be able to summon without assistance. Frequently, someone else has previously said what you want to say, and often he or she has said it with more specificity, in sharper and more precise language, or with a bite or sting you wish you had thought of. I doubt if there is anyone reading these words who has never, ever quoted someone else—we all do it. We all recite famous words and phrases. We also repeat anonymous or unattributed sentiments offered by friends and passersby.

These quotations bring all that and something extra: they are associated with the nation's oldest and largest—and arguably, most successful—civil rights organization, the ninety-two-year-old National Association for the Advancement of Colored People (NAACP).

The NAACP itself is proof of a famous quotation—W. E. B. DuBois's assertion in 1903 that "the problem of the Twentieth Century is the problem of the color line!" Begun in 1909 to fight racial discrimination, the NAACP today has twenty-two hundred branches scattered throughout the fifty states. Its more than six hundred thousand volunteers are the frontline troops for civil rights in their communities.

At the last century's beginning, NAACP membership cards could be death warrants in parts of the American South, so determined were the opponents of equality. But NAACP activists were more determined to win equality and perfect our democracy—this book records the words of many of them over the years. The organization's existence at age ninety-two is proof of its leaders' and members' tenacity—and sad proof of the persistence of discrimination.

Offering quotations here are women and men known and unknown, noted and nameless, famous and faceless—all of them fighters for expanded freedom. When race and pungent thought are combined in a well-turned phrase, lively reading and writing are the result.

Janet Cheatham Bell has collected material from widely scattered sources—NAACP organizational files and archives; histories of twentieth-century America, the American South, and the civil rights movement; collections of speeches and newspapers and magazines, including black publications until recently unknown to the general public.

Despite the seriousness of the central subject, not all the material is grim—or even challenging. Much of it is inspirational—these words come, after all, from a story of the steady triumph of right over wrong. Some of these are angry words— but anger is a proper emotion to bring to this fight. Some of the words are humorous—laughter is a frequently employed weapon that can win—and wound. And some are musical, lyrical—prose poetry from singers without any instrument except their voices or pens and their minds.

"Mastery of language affords remarkable power," Frantz Fanon said. That's a quote.

Between these covers are more—all of them powerful words.

JULIAN BOND, March 2001

JULIAN BOND.
Chairman, NAACP national board of directors

(Author's Collection)

1

<hr/>

Know Something to
Believe in Something

It is imperative that young people be told that we
have come a long way, otherwise they are likely to
become cynical. A cynical young person . . . means
that he or she has gone from knowing nothing to
believing in nothing.

Maya Angelou

When I was a teenager and a member of the Youth
Division of the NAACP, we picketed a supermarket
in Indianapolis that refused to hire blacks.

I joined the picket line again while studying at Indiana
University when the local NAACP branch was marching in
front of a barbershop near the Bloomington campus that
would not serve African-Americans. In both instances the
local branches were successful in eliminating racial discrimination. NAACP branches around the country have repeatedly
planned and carried out similar attacks on racism. And much
of the time their efforts have been effective because the

NAACP is relentless. *Shelley v. Kraemer* is a case in point. It took thirty-one years, but the NAACP won its battle against restrictive covenants—clauses in real estate deeds forbidding the sale of property to a buyer because of his race. In a unanimous decision the U.S. Supreme Court ruled in 1948 that such clauses were unconstitutional.

The title *Till Victory Is Won* is a phrase from the NAACP's official song, "Lift Every Voice and Sing." I use it here in homage to the NAACP's persistence. Although their tactics have changed as circumstances have dictated, the organization is committed to staying the course on this long journey to freedom and justice until victory is finally won.

AMERICAN APARTHEID

In a speech, Julian Bond, board chairman of the NAACP, reminded his audience, "American slavery was a human horror of staggering dimensions. It lasted twenty times longer than the Nazi holocaust, killed ten times as many people, and destroyed cultures on three continents. The profits it produced endowed great fortunes and enriched generations."

In 1909 when the NAACP was founded, only forty-four years had passed since slavery had officially been outlawed. Today, slavery's legacy—racism in all areas of American life—remains with us. Before the NAACP was up and running and for many years afterward, whites and blacks were not allowed to interact openly unless the black person was clearly perceived as being subservient. Everything—public transportation, education, restaurants, hotels, entertainment, neighborhoods, employment—was segregated by race. It was *apartheid*

American-style. In some states the segregation was supported by legislation; however, in those states without such laws, such as New York, where the NAACP was first established, the custom was just as rigidly enforced. It took incredible self-possession, commitment, and courage for the black and white founders and charter members to meet and work together in such an environment. Even after twenty-four years of intense effort by the NAACP, W. E. B. DuBois, a founder, wrote in the *Crisis,* their official journal, "There seems no hope that America in our day will yield in its color or race hatred any substantial ground."

The freedom of movement that African-Americans take for granted today is largely due to the perseverance of the NAACP. Admittedly, this is a work in progress, but the incremental changes have made a monumental difference.

Unexplored Wilderness

Most Americans, including African-Americans and especially the young, don't have any idea that the NAACP played such a pivotal role in American history. This is not common knowledge because to examine African-American history and the role of the NAACP is to talk about racism. And talking about racism is outside the American comfort zone, particularly in public and in interracial gatherings. Cornel West, the Harvard professor, puts it succinctly: "To talk about race in America is to explore the wilderness inside ourselves and to come to terms with a history that we'd rather conceal." When African-Americans are included in textbooks, film, and the news media, our story—past and present—is often distorted negatively. To spread the word of the proud accomplishments of the NAACP would diminish the myth of inept, sexually promiscuous, criminally inclined darkies who deserve their inferior status.

The young people who participate in the NAACP's Afro Academic, Cultural, Technological and Scientific Olympics (ACT-SO) are not the aimless, cynical ones whom Angelou refers to as "knowing nothing" and "believing in nothing"; they know their history and believe in themselves. Vernon Jarrett, from Chicago's Southside branch, created ACT-SO as a year-round enrichment program run by NAACP branches to stimulate and encourage high academic and cultural achievement among African-American high school students. *Till Victory Is Won* is dedicated to ACT-SO in celebration of their twenty-fifth anniversary and because they are the future of the NAACP and America.

LIVES ON THE LINE

While researching this book, I was deeply moved by the courage of countless NAACP members who have put their lives and livelihoods on the line—Walter White investigating lynchings, Septima Clark sticking to her principles and losing her career, Medgar Evers registering voters in Mississippi and losing his life. My admiration for the NAACP was renewed as I read about DuBois's unyielding defiance of anyone who would deny him his "full manhood rights" in an era when black men were lynched regularly with impunity. Then there was eventual Supreme Court justice Thurgood Marshall tirelessly traveling the country to defend black folk in malevolent courtrooms and not being certain if he would get home alive. To paraphrase Flo Kennedy, the New York attorney, racists weren't willing to die for racism, but they were certainly willing to kill for it.

I was astonished to learn *(cherchez la femme)* that it was a woman who had brought the passion and indignation of DuBois, William Monroe Trotter, and Ida B. Wells-Barnett of the all-black Niagara Movement together with the money and influence of the all-white National Negro Committee. That committee included Oswald Garrison Villard, William English Walling, Mary White Ovington, and others. Ovington, the persistent catalyst, an educated woman from one of New York's finer European American families, came to the new organization with an abolitionist heritage, as did Villard, the grandson of famed abolitionist William Lloyd Garrison. The two groups essentially merged to form the National Association for the Advancement of Colored People. Trotter and Wells-Barnett shortly became disillusioned with the pace and control set by the white leaders, but DuBois shrewdly understood that to build the widely effective organization he envisioned, ample financing was essential. And a people just two generations removed from being enslaved, and still laboring under fierce and systematic racial oppression that circumscribed every area of their lives, had the will but not the way to mount a sustained attack on that system.

THE NEXT LEVEL

Under the NAACP's long and relentless insistence that this country live up to its expressed ideals, it became decidedly more difficult to justify racial restrictions. Encouraged by former NAACP field director Ella Baker, college students took the baton and moved the struggle to another level with the direct action of freedom rides and sit-ins. Then the NAACP added affirmative action and economic boycotts to its traditional focus on legal redress. The fight has now moved from finding seats on buses and at lunch counters to seeking seats in government and on corporate boards. For the new century the NAACP's goals encompass not only protecting civil rights, but also promoting economic development and educational excellence, reaching out to young people and gaining more political power. These goals of the twenty-first century are used as categories by which this book is divided, presenting the words of a variety of NAACP officers, members, and award recipients. Each chapter includes a statement from various U.S. presidential administrations to provide a hint of the political environment in which the NAACP labored.

NEW LEADERSHIP

After several years of internal turmoil, the new national leadership team of Kweisi Mfume, president and CEO, and Julian Bond, chairman of the board, is restoring the organization's luster. The NAACP is a volunteer organization funded by membership dues and contributions. Some branches have paid staff, most do not. Fortunately the association has the powerful support of proud and independent black churches around the country. Julius C. Hope, national director of religious affairs, credits the organization's Youth Division and Religious Affairs Department for the strong showings at marches on the state capitals of Florida (in support of affirmative action in higher education) and South Carolina (against flying the Confederate battle flag). The two chief officers—Benjamin Hooks and Benjamin Chavis—immediately preceding Mfume were members of the clergy.

To make my own contribution to the NAACP, I decided to gather the wisdom of NAACP leaders, members, and award recipients—past and present—and share these words with the world. I have chosen the quotations for this look at the NAACP to present a range of ideas and perceptions and so that those most intimately involved with the organization could speak for themselves. Their words are defiant, controversial, provocative, and inspiring.

This collection is meant only to whet your appetite, so I have included a list of suggested further reading for those who want more. Please read, enjoy, be informed and inspired.

(l–r) ROY WILKINS, HENRY LEE MOON,
WALTER WHITE, THURGOOD MARSHALL, c. 1951

*(Library of Congress, Prints & Photographs Division, Visual Materials from the
NAACP records)*

2

---◆◆◆---

PROTECTING CIVIL RIGHTS

We are here to serve notice that we are in a fight to
the death for the rights guaranteed us as American
citizens by the Constitution.

JAMES WELDON JOHNSON (1871–1938),
field secretary, 1916–19; chief officer, 1920–30;
wrote lyrics for "Lift Every Voice and Sing"

The NAACP was established as an "aggressive watchdog
of Negro rights."

And that is exactly what the organization has been. The
major problem to be fought in the beginning was the lynching
of black men on the excuse that they had raped white women.
Tuskegee Institute in Alabama kept track of these mob mur-
ders after the Civil War, and for eighty-seven years, until 1952,
they reported lynchings every year. In 1911, the year the
NAACP was formally incorporated in New York City, sixty
blacks were known to have been lynched, down from sixty-
seven the year before.

In 1913, NAACP leaders were unsuccessful in their effort to persuade President Woodrow Wilson not to racially segregate the workplaces, rest rooms, and cafeterias of federal employees. Two years later they protested and boycotted the patently racist and historically inaccurate movie *Birth of a Nation,* but had little impact on its popularity.

There were some victories. In 1920, James Weldon Johnson was elected as the first black executive officer of the NAACP, and in 1935 a black became chairman of the board for the first time. He was Louis T. Wright, a hospital administrator and former surgeon for the New York Police Department. And in 1926 the NAACP was able to free Ossian Sweet. Dr. Sweet was a Detroit physician who had killed a member of a mob while defending his home and family after they had moved into a previously all-white neighborhood.

In 1947, thirty-eight years after the NAACP was established, Harry S. Truman was the first U.S. president to accept an invitation to speak at the annual convention. The following year Truman issued an executive order desegregating the armed forces.

The cause of lynching in the South is nothing less than the perpetration, especially by black men, of the hideous crime of rape.

THEODORE ROOSEVELT,
president of the United States, 1901–9
(1906 message to Congress)

INDIVIDUAL EFFORTS

To talk about race in America is to explore the wilderness inside ourselves and to come to terms with a history that we'd rather conceal.

CORNEL WEST, ACT-SO judge; philosopher,
activist, author, professor

———

The ideals and ambitions which the Negro entertains for himself are precisely those which the white man entertains for himself. And this the white man foolishly resents.

ARCHIBALD GRIMKÉ (1849–1930), founder;
president, Washington, D.C., branch, 1913–24;
diplomat and author; Spingarn Medal, 1919

When [A. Philip] Randolph stood there and talked that day, it made a different man of me. From that day on, I was determined that I was gonna fight for freedom until I was able to get some of it myself.

E. D. NIXON (1899–1987), president, Montgomery
branch, 1939–51; organized the 1955 bus boycott

———◆———

They can do what they can, but I'll never give in again.

FANNIE LOU HAMER (1917–77),
civil rights leader;
founder, Mississippi Freedom
Democratic Party

I felt that one had better die fighting against injustice than to die like a dog or a rat in a trap. I had already determined to sell my life as dearly as possible if attacked.

IDA B. WELLS-BARNETT (1862–1931),
founder; newspaper publisher and journalist,
antilynching crusader

—◆—

To act is to be committed, and to be committed is to be in danger.

JAMES BALDWIN (1924–87),
Image Award, 1980;
author and activist

It is a burden of black people that we have to do more than talk.

BARBARA JORDAN (1936–96),
Spingarn Medal, 1992;
congresswoman from Texas

———◆———

I can't imagine how knowing one's history would not urge one to be an activist.

JOHN HOPE FRANKLIN,
Spingarn Medal, 1995;
historian and author of
From Slavery to Freedom and other books

My mother viewed speaking impeccably proper English as a strategy in the overall battle for civil rights.

BEBE MOORE CAMPBELL, Image Award, 1995;
author of *Your Blues Ain't Like Mine*
and other novels

———◆———

You're acting all the time when you're black. Black people are acting out roles every day in this country just to keep on getting by.

MILES DAVIS (1926–91),
Image Award, 1989; award-winning
trumpet player and composer

I took the energy it takes to pout [about racism] and wrote some blues.

DUKE (EDWARD KENNEDY) ELLINGTON
(1899–1974), Spingarn Medal, 1959;
jazz musician and composer

———— ✦ ————

The day I become content is the day I cease to be anything more than a man who hit home runs. I might not feel this way if I weren't black. . . . See, I'm one of the lucky ones. I could do something that white people would pay to see. . . . But what about all the black teachers and mechanics and carpenters and janitors and waitresses? . . . I have a moral responsibility to do whatever I can.

HANK (HENRY) AARON. Spingarn Medal, 1975;
board of trustees; Hall of Fame baseball player
and holder of the career home-run record

I don't like to be mistreated. I don't like to see other people mistreated. I believe in fighting back.

ROY WILKINS (1901–81),
executive director, 1955–77;
Spingarn Medal, 1964

I didn't get up [from my seat on the bus]. I was tired of giving in to white people.

ROSA PARKS, branch secretary,
Montgomery, Alabama, 1943–57;
Spingarn Medal, 1979; founder, Rosa and
Raymond Parks Institute for Self-Development

We cannot stand still; we cannot permit ourselves simply to be victims.

W. E. B. DuBois (1868–1963), founder;
Crisis editor, 1910–34;
Spingarn Medal, 1920

———•———

Meeting hate with hate and anger with anger only poisons your own being and has no effect on your enemies.

Medgar W. Evers (1925–63),
field secretary, Mississippi, 1954–63;
Spingarn Medal, 1963

It does not mean that because we do not hate that we do not fight.

LILLIE CARROLL JACKSON (1889–1975),
president, Baltimore branch, 1935–70;
board member; activist and educator

———•———

If a black person gets in trouble, he calls out two names, Jesus and the NAACP.

JOE MADISON, member, national board;
former branch president, Detroit;
morning talk-radio host, Washington, D.C.

GROUP STRUGGLES

The race problem in the United States has resolved itself into a question of saving black men's bodies and white men's souls.

JAMES WELDON JOHNSON (1871–1938),
field secretary, 1916–19; chief officer, 1920–30; wrote
lyrics for official song, "Lift Every Voice and Sing"

———◆———

Until the killing of black mothers' sons becomes as important to the rest of the country as the killing of white mothers' sons, we who believe in freedom cannot rest.

ELLA BAKER (1903–86),
assistant field secretary, 1941–43;
director of branches, 1943–46

We must understand that racism is detrimental to all of us, not only to black people, but to all Americans.

JULIUS C. HOPE. national director,
Religious Affairs Department;
pastor, New Grace Baptist Church, Detroit

———

Freedom is never granted; it is won. Justice is never given; it is exacted.

A. PHILIP RANDOLPH (1889–1979),
Spingarn Medal, 1942; founder, Brotherhood of
Sleeping Car Porters international union

The government they devised was defective from the start, requiring several amendments, a civil war, and momentous social transformation to attain . . . respect for the individual freedoms and human rights we hold as fundamental today.

THURGOOD MARSHALL (1908–93),
director, Legal Defense and Educational Fund,
1936–61; Spingarn Medal, 1946;
U.S. Supreme Court justice, 1967–91

———◆———

Should we accept a Jim Crow institution, however deluxe, or should we make the far harder decision of insisting on complete integration? [We decided that] second-class status must never be accepted.

WALTER WHITE (1893–1955),
executive secretary, 1931–55;
Spingarn Medal, 1937

Forcing change takes two things: pressure and negotiation. You try to negotiate away injustice. If negotiations fail, you apply pressure.

CHARLES EVERS, field secretary,
Mississippi, 1963–69; former mayor,
Fayette, Mississippi

———◆———

The fact that you attempt to keep [black] people down shows there is something in them that you fear, namely that given a chance, black people would show their equality with whites.

ARCHIBALD GRIMKÉ (1849-1930), founder;
president, Washington, D.C., branch, 1913–24;
diplomat and author; Spingarn Medal, 1919

Segregation was constitutional [in 1947]. It was also hogging and shunning. White people hogged every good thing. . . . And they made it clear that they wanted no part of blacks, except that little tiny piece that could be servile.

ROGER WILKINS. chairman,
Crisis Publishing Company; history professor

———◆———

Waiting is a sentence, not a solution.

ROY WILKINS (1901–81),
executive director, 1955–77;
Spingarn Medal, 1964

My personal problem with what is called "the sixties," roughly that period between the *Brown* decision of the Supreme Court (1954) and the election of Richard Nixon (1968), is that I think we won.

NIKKI GIOVANNI. Image Award, 1997;
poet and professor

———

Fortunately, the tide of progress moves in spite of the opposition.

CLARENCE MITCHELL JR. (1911–84),
Spingarn Medal, 1969;
director, Washington bureau, 1950–78

We still have not determined that America is for everybody.

ALTHEA T. L. SIMMONS (1924–90),
director, Washington bureau, 1978–90

———•———

We no longer have Jim Crow to battle, but . . . improving the lives of the black poor is the unfinished business of the civil rights movement.

VICTORIA L. VALENTINE,
editor in chief, *The Crisis*

People cry for justice as though it is easy to comprehend. It is not. It is difficult to dish up consistently.

RALPH WILEY, member;
author of *Why Black People Tend to Shout*
and other books

———◆———

You cannot erase in thirty years what it took two hundred years to establish.

DAISY BATES (1914–99), Spingarn Medal
(with the Little Rock Nine), 1958;
state president, Arkansas; journalist

Black people get their moral authority in this country not simply because they have suffered, but because they understand the suffering of other people in this world.

ELEANOR HOLMES NORTON, member,
Washington, D.C.; law professor

———❖———

Through the centuries of despair and dislocation, we had been creative, because we faced down death by daring to hope.

MAYA ANGELOU, Spingarn Medal, 1994;
Image Award, 1997; author and poet

A lesser people—I mean a people of weaker constitution and fortitude—would have given up on this country long ago. But we didn't. We are going to force this country to live up to what it is supposed to be about or we'll die in the attempt.

BARBARA JORDAN (1936–96),
Spingarn Medal, 1992; congresswoman from Texas

———◆———

The issues of African-Americans remain of foremost concern for the [NAACP], but Hispanics, Native Americans, and Asians . . . like us . . . live under the social limitations of not being white.

KWEISI MFUME, president and CEO since 1996;
represented Baltimore in U.S. Congress, 1986–96

No movement committed to long-term transformation and justice can afford to become overly dependent on [any] single strategy.

LANI GUINIER. Legal Defense and Educational Fund, 1981–89; law professor

———

We have to keep in mind that when we talk about civil rights, we are talking about those fundamental liberties that the Constitution guarantees.

CLARENCE MITCHELL JR. (1911–84), Spingarn Medal, 1969; director, Washington bureau, 1950–78

The struggle is far from over. There is much more to be said and much more to be done.

HARRY BELAFONTE. Chairman's Award, 1999
Image Awards; singer, actor, producer, activist

—◆—

VERNON JARRETT AND ACT-SO SCIENCE WINNERS
visit the National Aeronautics and Space Administration in 2000.

(Photo courtesy of NASA)

3

ACHIEVING EDUCATIONAL
EXCELLENCE

People who think education is expensive have never
counted the cost of ignorance.

ANDREW YOUNG, Spingarn Medal, 1978;
former mayor of Atlanta

Close to half a century after the NAACP successfully
argued before the U.S. Supreme Court for the 1954
decision to abolish legal segregation in public education, resis-
tance to equal educational opportunity remains intact.

We have moved from schools segregated by law to schools
segregated by practice. And the separate facilities are not
equal, as resources and funding are concentrated in wealthier
suburban communities. Urban schools, attended predomi-
nantly by minority students, are underfunded and understaffed.
These inadequate schools with few resources and often disin-
terested teachers have drained African-American aspirations

to educational achievement, creating internal barriers and stultifying ambition. The fight for equal opportunity in education has had to be joined to a fight to regenerate hope and to renew a tradition of excellence.

The gap in educational achievement that we expected school desegregation to close has apparently widened, but it can be eradicated. With parental involvement and the vigilance of community organizations like the NAACP, black students are being prepared to be high-achieving, productive citizens. The NAACP's efforts include national opposition to the school-voucher movement and a number of programs to promote educational excellence implemented by branches around the country. These initiatives include Back to School/Stay in School, the Reginald Lewis Youth Entrepreneurship Institute, and ACT-SO. The Lewis Institute teaches the fundamentals of owning and operating a business to high school students and also assists them in developing a business plan they can use to secure funding. For more about ACT-SO, see chapter 5, "Reaching Youth."

I have today issued an Executive Order directing the use of troops under federal authority to aid in the execution of federal law at Little Rock, Arkansas.

DWIGHT D. EISENHOWER, president of the
United States, 1953–61
(September 25, 1957, to control the raging mob that
was preventing the desegregation of
Central High School)

Obstacles to Education

Segregationists were right. The fatal flaw in their system was education. If they wanted to preserve [segregation] forever, they should never have allowed us to be educated.

> AARON HENRY (1922–97), founder, Coahoma
> County, Mississippi, branch, 1953;
> state president, 1960–94;
> state legislator, 1979–93

———

Our humanity is served back to us through the eyes of those who have diminished us. And they serve back . . . a view of ourselves that is incomplete. If we don't look to the bigger picture, our view will narrow to that which is constantly fed to us.

> SIDNEY POITIER, Image Award Hall of Fame,
> 2001; film actor, director, producer

We can never expect the public schools to teach us
as much about our history as we want to know.

JOHN HOPE FRANKLIN. Spingarn Medal, 1995;
historian and author of
From Slavery to Freedom
and other books

———◆———

Separate [students] by color and they grow up without learning the tremendous truth that it is impossible to judge the mind of a man by the color of his
face. Is there any truth that America needs to learn
more?

W. E. B. DuBois (1868–1963), founder;
Crisis editor, 1910–34; Spingarn Medal, 1920

The [U.S.] Supreme Court had given us a beautifully wrapped gift [in the 1954 school desegregation decision], but when we removed the shiny wrappings, the box was empty.

AARON HENRY (1922–97), founder Coahoma
County, Mississippi, branch, 1953;
state president, 1960–94; state legislator, 1979–95

———•———

Although it's no longer against the law [to teach blacks to read], someone, somehow, still makes sure that you don't know how to read, because if you can read, you can unlock information and you're better able to understand the forces that are oppressing you.

AUGUST WILSON. Theater Award, 1992;
author of *Two Trains Running*, *Fences*,
and other plays

A lot of learning has lost its play and has become very concrete, very literal, very exacting. . . . In our schools, students are mostly trained to get to the answer quickly. Part of teaching is helping students learn how to tolerate ambiguity, consider possibilities, and ask questions that are unanswerable.

SARA LAWRENCE LIGHTFOOT. member;
education professor and author of
The Good High School and other books

———◆———

It is the duty of education at every level to care about the opportunity for children of limited resources to establish an intimate relationship with ideas and high ideals.

RUTH SIMMONS. member; president,
Brown University, Providence, Rhode Island

Students are not sent to school to learn to obey. They are sent there to learn to do, to think, to execute, to be men and women.

W. E. B. DuBois (1868–1963), founder; *Crisis* editor, 1910–34; Spingarn Medal, 1920

———◆———

There is a problem with disparity when you've got seventeen new prisons on the construction block and not one dime for school construction.

Hilary O. Shelton, director of the Washington bureau since 1997

It's irresponsible to tell children to be successful but not empower them with the tools they need.

JEFFREY JOHNSON,
national coordinator of youth councils

———•———

EXCELLENCE IN EDUCATION

Though you will be surrounded by those who say that education doesn't count or excellence doesn't matter, believe me, they do. . . . Hard work produces good results. Dumb people run absolutely nothing.

L. DOUGLAS WILDER. Spingarn Medal, 1990;
first African-American elected
governor of Virginia, 1989

———————

No one else can retrieve our values and salvage our people better than we can.

DOROTHY I. HEIGHT. Spingarn Medal, 1993;
former CEO, National Council of Negro Women

Everything I need to get over in this world is inside . . . connecting me to everybody and everything that's ever been . . . . I can't live inside yesterday's pain, but I can't live without it.

> GEORGE C. WOLFE. Theater Award, 1988;
> author of *Colored Museum* and other plays;
> director

———

You don't get in life what you want; you get in life what you are.

> LES BROWN. member; motivational speaker
> and author of *Live Your Dreams* and
> *It's Not Over Until You Win*

You keep on pushing in life just as you do in science. You ask the questions, check the results for accuracy, then move forward.

DARIUS HOLLINGS, ACT-SO gold medal in
science, 1993

———◆———

I was one hundred percent behind the proposed higher standards [for athletes]. . . . I urged that we should either get serious about academic standards or cut out the hypocrisy and pay college athletes as professionals.

ARTHUR ASHE (1943–93), member; author of the
four-volume sports history *A Hard Road to Glory;*
champion tennis player

The healthiest competition occurs when average people win by putting in above average effort.

COLIN POWELL. Spingarn Medal, 1991;
U.S. secretary of state since 2001;
retired general, U.S. army

—•—

Sometimes you think you're the only one doing well in a particular subject until you come across a program like ACT-SO and find there are many young, talented blacks doing equally as well academically.

ROBERT JONES. ACT-SO first prize
in chemistry, 1987

After one has discovered what he is made for, he should surrender all of the power in his being to the achievement of this.

MARTIN LUTHER KING JR. (1929–68),
Spingarn Medal, 1957; civil rights leader

———◆———

No matter how good they say you are, always keep working on your game.

MICHAEL JORDAN. Image Award, 1999;
businessman, basketball player

———◆———

[When] you're a black woman in film, you have to look hard for risks to take; otherwise, you'll be mediocre.

HALLE BERRY. Image Award, 2000;
actress, producer

When I went to the playground, I never picked the best players. I picked guys with less talent, but who were willing to work hard, who had the desire to be great.

MAGIC (EARVIN) JOHNSON.
Image Award, 1992;
businessman, former basketball player

———❖———

While everyone else is sleeping, I'm working.

WILL SMITH. Image Award, 1999; rap artist, actor

In my career, I found the most important thing is not to be self-conscious about [race] and not to let it interfere with the way you think or the manner in which you operate.

REGINALD LEWIS (1942–93),
CEO and major shareholder, TLC Beatrice
International Holdings, Inc.;
lawyer, financier, and philanthropist

————◆————

You can entertain people and give them a little information at the same time. Your mind doesn't stop working when you become an actor.

WHOOPI GOLDBERG. Image Award, 1988;
actress, producer of *Hollywood Squares*
and other television programs

I am trying to get our people to see that their color does not hold them back as much as [the way] they think.

GEORGE WASHINGTON CARVER (1864–1943),
Spingarn Medal, 1923;
research botanist at Tuskegee Institute

———•———

Excellence is the best deterrent to racism.

JESSE JACKSON, Spingarn Medal, 1989;
international human rights leader

We have to change the erroneous assumption that you have a better chance to be Magic Johnson than you do of being a brain surgeon.

HENRY LOUIS GATES JR., member; chair,
W. E. B. DuBois Institute for
Afro-American Studies, Harvard

—◆—

Reading gave me hope. For me It was the open door.

OPRAH WINFREY, Spingarn Medal, 2000;
Image Award, 1995; host and owner of
The Oprah Winfrey Show

My people were right to expect that if an opportunity were open one of our own should not be bypassed. But . . . a Negro must qualify on musical grounds and must be equal to the best competition if he is to find a place.

MARIAN ANDERSON (1902–93),
Spingarn Medal, 1939; concert singer

There were things I wanted to do [in music] that were not in books, and I had to ask a lot of questions. I was always lucky enough to run into people who had the answers.

DUKE (EDWARD KENNEDY) ELLINGTON
(1899–1974), Spingarn Medal, 1959;
jazz musician and composer

Education is a lifelong process. It has a beginning and no end.

PATRICIA RUSSELL-MCCLOUD. member;
president, Russell-McCloud & Associates, Atlanta;
professional orator and author

———•———

Organized education gives us general information, but there are things we have to learn by ourselves.

LAURYN HILL. President's Award,
Image Awards, 1999; rap musician, actress

[ACT-SO] competitions are more than just winning and losing. It has helped me to improve my work.

KERN BRUCE. ACT-SO participant,
Newark, New Jersey

———◆———

Always know there is unlimited power in a developed mind and a disciplined spirit. If your mind can conceive it and your heart can believe it, you can achieve it.

JESSE JACKSON. Spingarn Medal, 1989;
international human rights leader

I leave you a thirst for education. More and more, Negroes are taking full advantage of hard-won opportunities for learning and the educational level of the Negro population is at its highest level in history.

MARY MCLEOD BETHUNE (1875–1955),
Spingarn Medal, 1935; founder and president,
Bethune-Cookman College,
Daytona Beach, Florida

MADAM C. J. WALKER
(front, center), entrepeneuer, with her sales agents in Ohio, c. 1918

(A'Lelia Bundles / Walker Family Collection)

4

---⟫◆⟪---

Nurturing Economic
Development

To be a poor man is hard, but to be a poor race in the
land of dollars is the very bottom of hardships.

W. F. B. DuBois (1868–1963), founder;
Crisis editor, 1910–34; Spingarn Medal, 1920

Once the efforts of the civil rights movement had managed to remove legal barriers to public accommodations, it became apparent that many African-Americans were not economically prepared to take advantage of the restaurants, travel, and other opportunities that were available.

Economic parity had to be the next fight, and affirmative action in employment became one of the most effective weapons in that fight. In 1941, President Franklin Roosevelt had issued, under pressure from the NAACP, Executive Order 8802, banning employment discrimination in industries holding government contracts for war production and job training in war industries. This order allowed a number of blacks and women to be employed in places where they had previously not been allowed to work.

Building and supporting black businesses and boycotting businesses with discriminatory practices are other tools utilized in this ongoing struggle. Recent NAACP programs that have had an economic impact include an agreement with the Small Business Administration to deliver $1.4 billion in loan assistance to African-American entrepreneurs and a partnership with Fannie Mae, the largest source of funding for home mortgages, to expand financing for home ownership to minority families.

Recognizing that media images are a prime influence on how blacks are perceived by the masses of people in contemporary society, the NAACP criticized major television networks for their failure to include African-Americans in significant roles in their 1999 programming. As a result, early in 2000, the NAACP signed agreements with Fox, CBS, NBC, and ABC to adopt a series of initiatives to increase opportunities for people of color in all network operations. These unprecedented agreements should create more jobs for blacks in the entertainment industry, both in front of and behind the camera.

The job of ending discrimination in this country is not done. . . . We should reaffirm the principle of Affirmative Action and fix the practices. . . . Mend it, but don't end it.

BILL (WILLIAM JEFFERSON) CLINTON,
president of the United States, 1993–2001

PERSONAL FINANCE

While many believe that only the wealthy have economic power, all of us have the power to spend our money where we choose, whether we're making a million-dollar purchase or buying a box of detergent.

CAMILLE COSBY. member;
philanthropist and author

Nothing is free. Like these little programs that the government got. . . . It costs your everything. 'Cause once you go in to get food stamps or a welfare check, if you had any secret, you don't have it when you leave there.

CORA LEE JOHNSON. member,
Soperton, Georgia; chair,
Rural Black Women's Leadership Project

One major weakness of the sharecropping system . . . was the white man's failure to recognize the factor that could destroy this [economic] bondage—education.

AARON HENRY (1922–97), founder, Coahoma County, Mississippi, branch, 1953; state president, 1960–94; state legislator, 1979–95

———◆———

You've got to kid white folks along. When you're depending on 'em for a living, make 'em *think* you like it.

LANGSTON HUGHES (1902–67), Spingarn Medal, 1960; poet and author

A fight for antilynching legislation without just as vigorous a battle for economic independence is to fight the manifestation of the evil and ignore its cause.

CHARLES HAMILTON HOUSTON (1895–1950),
Spingarn Medal, 1950;
chief legal counsel, 1935–38; law professor

———◦———

The sooner we're able to diminish white supremacy, then the sooner the [economic] gap is going to narrow and disappear.

JULIAN BOND, board chair since 1998; president,
Atlanta branch, 1973–87; former Georgia legislator;
civil rights professor

While I believe that people do not live by bread alone, they certainly have to have bread.

HOLSEY O. HICKMAN, member, Dallas, Texas

———

The most menial job is never beneath our dignity, but rather an opportunity to love and serve joyfully.

SUSAN L. TAYLOR, ACT-SO judge; senior vice president and publication director, Essence Communications

You have to make sacrifices in order to make progress.

MEDGAR W. EVERS (1925–63),
field secretary, Mississippi, 1954–63;
Spingarn Medal, 1963

People create their own luck by the choices they make.

BENJAMIN S. CARSON SR., member;
pediatric neurosurgeon, Baltimore

Affirmative action opens up opportunities, it does not lower standards.

JOHN HOPE FRANKLIN. Spingarn Medal, 1995; historian and author of *From Slavery to Freedom* and other books

———◆———

A society that has done something special *against* the Negro for hundreds of years must now do something special *for* him.

MARTIN LUTHER KING JR. (1929–68), Spingarn Medal, 1957; civil rights leader

In America we must still think about reparations, because there are thirty million blacks whose lives have been devastated as a result of segregation and slavery.

LEON HOWARD SULLIVAN (1922–2001), Spingarn Medal, 1971; founder, Opportunities Industrialization Centers (OIC); president, International Foundation for Education and Self-Help (IFESH)

The growth of the African-American middle class means that in husband-wife families with both working outside the home, blacks have almost gained parity with whites in income but not in wealth.

MARY FRANCES BERRY, member; chair, U.S. Commission on Civil Rights; author and history professor

Politics don't control the world; money does.

ANDREW YOUNG. Spingarn Medal, 1978;
former mayor of Atlanta

———•———

BUSINESS FINANCE

I was tired of making money for other people, so I went into business for myself.

LEE McCORD. member;
business owner, Chicago, Illinois

———✦———

Money is America's god and businesspeople can dig black power if it coincides with green power.

JACKIE ROBINSON (1919–72),
Spingarn Medal, 1956;
businessman, baseball player

When the theatricality, the entertainment value, the marketing of life is complete, we will find ourselves living not in a nation but in a consortium of industries, and wholly unintelligible to ourselves.

TONI MORRISON. Image Award, 1998;
Nobel laureate in literature, 1993

———•———

The bottom line is you have to make money. Then nobody cares what color you are.

QUINCY JONES. Image Award, 1990;
musician, multimedia mogul

We don't have to be entertainers, athletes, or drug dealers to make money in this country. . . . The great fortunes are made in business.

MACEO SLOAN. member;
entrepreneur, Durham, North Carolina

———◆———

If you believe in something, to have the commitment is really more important than having the money.

JOHN H. JOHNSON. Spingarn Medal, 1966;
CEO, Johnson Publishing Company

The girls and women of our race must not be afraid to take hold of business endeavor and, by patient industry, close economy, determined effort and close application to business, wring success out of a number of business opportunities that lie at their very doors.

MADAM C. J. WALKER (1867–1919), member;
major financial supporter;
founder of hair-care products business

———◆———

When you're running a successful business, you tend to stay with the existing formula. But you can't stand still . . . you have to say that the objective is to win.

KENNETH I. CHENAULT. member;
president, American Express Company

I think from success you'll gain access. . . . I don't think black folks need unity as much as they need industry. . . . [W]e have to start opening businesses.

KEENEN IVORY WAYANS. Image Award, 1990;
producer, actor, director

———•◆•———

The most exhilarating, exciting, and empowering business experience you can have is being an entrepreneur.

EARL G. GRAVES. Spingarn Medal, 1999;
publisher, *Black Enterprise* magazine

If you live a life of service, you don't have to worry about money. Money will come.

ROBERT SHAW LOGAN. member; president,
Logan Enterprises, Saluda, South Carolina

———•—•———

People who [played] a role in running the city and state . . . used their clout to develop economic opportunities for blacks.

PERCY E. SUTTON. Spingarn Medal, 1987;
chairman emeritus, Inner City Broadcasting,
New York City

[Royalties earned for writing lyrics] was sweeter than money merely worked for. This was money gained for materializing the intangible.

JAMES WELDON JOHNSON (1871–1938),
field secretary, 1916–19; chief officer, 1920–30;
wrote lyrics for official song,
"Lift Every Voice and Sing"

Income is not greenbacks, it is satisfaction; it is creation; it is beauty.

W. E. B. DUBOIS (1868–1963),
founder; *Crisis* editor, 1910–34;
Spingarn Medal, 1920

SHARING THE WEALTH

My object in life is not simply to make money for myself or to spend it on myself. I love to use a part of what I make in trying to help others.

MADAM C. J. WALKER (1867–1919) member;
major financial supporter;
founder of hair-care products business

——•——

What I know for sure is that what you give comes back to you. . . . Life is an energy exchange of giving and receiving, and the way you have what you want is to give what you need. I happen to love giving. . . . Always have.

OPRAH WINFREY, Spingarn Medal, 2000;
Image Award, 1995; host and owner of
The Oprah Winfrey Show

It's better to be about something and get nothing for it than to be about nothing and get something.

BRYAN STEVENSON. member; law professor; director, Equal Justice Initiative, Montgomery, Alabama

<hr />

Once I stopped dwelling on what I didn't have, on what I thought I was going to lose, and began to give freely, everything began to flow into my life.

PATTI LABELLE. Image Award, 1992; singer, actress, author

I always wanted to do things for people. That's my motto—that's my religion.

GLADYS WOODARD (1912–99),
branch president, Detroit; founder and director,
Delray United Action Council

We must want to do more than merely survive, we must want to succeed. Our greatest challenge is to remember who we are—the people who refused to die—and to do the work.

SUSAN L. TAYLOR, ACT-SO judge; senior vice
president and publication director,
Essence Communications

The widening gulf between rich and poor is evident, but there seems to be no coherent, effective, popular alternative to the dominant free-trade ideology that values the needs of multinational corporations over those of the earth's majority.

CLAYBORNE CARSON, member; director and senior editor of the Martin Luther King Jr. Papers Project, Stanford University

It dawned on me that we are not going to be ultimately successful in the world until we close this economic gap between blacks and whites, not just here in the United States but around the world.

RANDALL ROBINSON, member; president and executive director, TransAfrica, Washington, D.C.

Economic empowerment is the logical extension of the civil rights movement. Without the resources to take care of ourselves, we will forever remain dependent.

KWEISI MFUME, president and CEO since 1996; represented Baltimore in U.S. Congress, 1986–96

KWEISI MFUME,

NAACP president and CEO, encourages young people
to be and do their best.

(Photo by Paul A. Green)

5

REACHING YOUTH

In the treatment of the child, the world foreshadows
its own future and faith.

W. E. B. DU BOIS (1868–1963), founder; *Crisis* editor,
1910–34; Spingarn Medal, 1920

The NAACP's Youth and College Division is the largest
organization of African-American young people in the
country.

Branches of the division conduct a number of programs
and events around the country. The Boston University branch
held a Civil Rights Film Series to discuss the historical context
of the films *4 Little Girls, Panther, Malcolm X,* and *Rosewood.*
The Medgar Evers College branch in New York City had a
College Survival Workshop for high school students. In 2000,
fifty thousand of these young activists and other NAACP
members marched in Tallahassee, Florida, to protest Governor

Jeb Bush's attack on affirmative action in higher education.

In 1977 the Afro Academic, Cultural, Technological and Scientific Olympics (ACT-SO), founded by Vernon Jarrett, was established by the NAACP as a year-round enrichment program designed to recruit, stimulate, improve, and encourage high academic and cultural achievement among African-American high school students. Students compete in twenty-four categories for scholarship money and other prizes. Over the years a great many of these young achievers have gone on to magnificent careers in a variety of fields.

To keep its future and youngest members safe, the NAACP has joined with General Motors and the National Safe Kids Campaign to provide car seats for families with modest incomes. And Women in the NAACP (WIN) has a number of programs aimed at children including raising funds in collaboration with women in Ghana, West Africa, in efforts to construct an early-childhood education center in Ghana.

[The Justice Department is] not going to compel children who don't choose to have an integrated education to have one.

WILLIAM BRADFORD REYNOLDS.
assistant attorney general for civil rights in the
administration of Ronald Reagan,
president of the United States, 1981–89

PREPARING FOR LIFE

I have come to realize that what distinguishes one child from another is not ability, but access. Access to education, access to opportunity, access to love.

LAURYN HILL. President's Award, Image Awards, 1999; rap musician, actress

———◆———

Enhancing the self-image and self-respect of black children [is] one of my main priorities.

ALVIN POUSSAINT. member, Boston, Massachusetts; psychiatrist and professor of psychiatry

In knowing how to overcome little things, a centimeter at a time, gradually when bigger things come, you're prepared.

KATHERINE DUNHAM. Image Award Hall of
Fame, 1990; director of the Dunham Center for the
Performing Arts, Southern Illinois University

———◆———

Teach our young people where they've been so that they'll have aspirations for where they can go.

SHANNON REEVES. branch president,
Oakland, California

Young people are looking for direction and inspiration. Adults have to believe in the potential of young people and turn that into substantive support and encouragement.

HIEWET SENGHOR, national director,
Youth and College Division

———•———

ACT-SO lets kids know that there is nothing on the earth that they can't do.

TERRENCE BRADFORD TARVER,
ACT-SO gold medal in classical and
contemporary vocal music, 1998

All work is honorable. Always do your best because someone is watching.

COLIN POWELL, Spingarn Medal, 1991;
U.S. secretary of state since 2001;
retired general, U.S. army

———•———

Help your children develop a passion in life. . . . They need an abiding interest to occupy their minds and keep them from the many devastating temptations of our society.

MYRLIE EVERS-WILLIAMS,
board chair, 1995–98; Spingarn Medal, 1998

Most of us grow up as quickly as we have to, getting further away by the day from who we were when we were children. We shorten our sails, temper our ambitions, and set aside our fondest expectations in order to face the day.

OSSIE DAVIS. Image Award, 1989;
actor, director, playwright

———◆———

You have to expect things of yourself before you can do them.

MICHAEL JORDAN. Image Award, 1999;
businessman, basketball player

Young people should never accept a limit on their horizons. . . . Learn everything there is to know.

GORDON PARKS, Spingarn Medal, 1972; author, photographer, musician

———◆———

ACT-SO [is] . . . a chance for our children to understand that they are bright, that they can achieve academically, and that as a community we will celebrate their efforts.

RHONDA K. WILSON, national director, ACT-SO

Being around other black students who were talented in many areas . . . gave me a sense of hope
[and inspired me] to study harder and do better.

ROY HARGROVE. ACT-SO gold medal, 1988;
jazz musician

———

I come to ACT-SO every year to be empowered and
inspired by . . . young people.

CORNEL WEST. ACT-SO judge; philosopher,
activist, author, professor

Younger people keep you edgy, but older people give you comfort.

NIKKI GIOVANNI, Image Award, 1997;
poet and professor

———◆———

The journey is not one generation. Each of us is an accumulated effort unfolding.

SIDNEY POITIER, Image Award Hall of Fame,
2001; film actor, director, producer

The best education I received was in the NAACP.

TANANARIVE DUE. ACT-SO gold medals, 1980,
1982; Miami youth council president, 1981;
author of *My Soul to Keep* and other novels

———◆———

[The young people] are not from our tradition.
They believe in NAACP values, but are able to see
beyond traditional approaches.

HAZEL DUKES. president, New York state
conference; former national president

If we tell our children that nothing has changed, then we cannot prepare them for the struggle, for who wants to struggle if the struggle is in vain?

BENJAMIN L. HOOKS,
executive director, 1977–93;
Baptist minister, lawyer,
and former member of the
Federal Communications Commission

———•———

Losing is the hardest thing to do . . . but to truly be a good winner you have to . . . understand the anguish of losing.

KWEISI MFUME, president and CEO since 1996;
represented Baltimore in U.S. Congress, 1986–96

You can talk all you want about individual behavior, but we incarcerate poor kids for things that middle-class kids get counseling for.

CONNIE (CONSTANCE L.) RICE,
former counsel, western region Legal Defense and
Educational Fund; attorney, Los Angeles

───◆───

African-Americans make up 13 percent of the ten-to-seventeen-year-old age group. Yet they make up 50 percent of all the juveniles transferred into adult courts . . . and 70 percent of juveniles transferred into adult prisons.

HILARY O. SHELTON, director of the
Washington bureau since 1997

Right now the number one construction in the United States is . . . prisons because there are some people who don't know what to do with young men and women who look like you. And if *you* don't make a decision about what's going to happen to young men and women who look like you, somebody else is.

VERNON JARRETT. ACT-SO founder, board
member; columnist, activist

———◆———

You don't need blackface in the twenty-first century to make a minstrel show.

SPIKE (SHELTON) LEE. Image Award, 1994;
filmmaker, director, actor

PREPARING FOR A LIVELIHOOD

The courage to create is a monumental thing, because every time you morph or expand to create, you leave something behind.

LAURENCE FISHBURNE, Image Award, 1999;
actor

I think hip-hop is a result of our young people [being] denied access to music in their public schools. When you take the instrumentation away, you are left with voices. . . . And they have a right to sing their song.

VASHTI MURPHY MCKENZIE, member;
African Methodist Episcopal bishop; former pastor,
Payne Memorial Church, Baltimore

You will find it the fashion in the America where eventually you will live and work, to judge . . . life's work by the amount of money it brings you. This is a grave mistake. The return from your work must be the satisfaction which that work brings you.

W. E. B. DuBois (1868–1963), founder;
Crisis editor, 1910–34; Spingarn Medal, 1920

———

If you fall in love with what you do, you will never work again.

John H. Johnson. Spingarn Medal, 1966;
CEO, Johnson Publishing Company

I pounded pavements, went to every audition. That was my spirit. Work at whatever you do, whether you get paid or not.

DEBBIE ALLEN, Image Award, 1994;
choreographer, dancer, actress, producer, and director

———

There is no paycheck that can equal the feeling of contentment that comes from being the person you are meant to be.

OPRAH WINFREY, Spingarn Medal, 2000;
Image Award, 1995; host and owner of
The Oprah Winfrey Show

You can never be great at anything unless you love it.

MAYA ANGELOU. Spingarn Medal, 1994; Image Award, 1997; author and poet

———◆———

Hard work is when you're doing something you don't want to do.

DENZEL WASHINGTON. Image Award, 1990; actor, philanthropist

Something which we think is impossible now is not impossible in another decade.

CONSTANCE BAKER MOTLEY, Legal Defense
and Educational Fund, 1946–64; federal judge

———◆———

I always advise young people to dream small dreams, because small dreams can be achieved. If you are going to travel a long distance, you can't burden yourself with a heavy load.

JOHN H. JOHNSON, Spingarn Medal, 1966;
CEO, Johnson Publishing Company

The world has improved mostly because unortho-dox people did unorthodox things. Not surprisingly, they had the courage and daring to think they could make a difference.

RUBY DEE. Image Award, 1999; actress and
author of *My One Good Nerve*

Life will mean much, much more to you when you are fighting for a cause than it possibly can if you . . . just make money. You'll stagnate and eventually die mentally.

LOUIS T. WRIGHT (1891–1952),
Spingarn Medal, 1940;
elected board chairman in 1935; physician

Every intersection in the road of life is an opportunity to make a decision, and at some I had only to listen.

DUKE (EDWARD KENNEDY) ELLINGTON
(1899–1974), Spingarn Medal, 1959;
jazz musician and composer

———◆———

I want [my daughter] to see that the biggest thing . . . is liking your black self and other people who look like you, and . . . that *black* and *lack* are not synonymous.

BENILDE LITTLE. Image Award, 1997;
author of *Good Hair* and *The Itch*

I want to feel that I made choices that empowered me as a human being. My career is going to be here and gone, but I'm always going to be a human being.

DANNY GLOVER. Image Award, 1994; actor

———

If you don't live the only life you have, you won't live some other life; you won't live any life at all.

JAMES BALDWIN (1924–87),
Image Award, 1980; author and activist

If my life stands for anything, it's that you can make it in this country, despite all the obstacles.

JOHNNIE L. COCHRAN JR., member;
attorney at law

———◆———

Mistakes are a fact of life. It's the response to the error that counts.

NIKKI GIOVANNI, Image Award, 1997;
poet and professor

———◆———

You can so outlive your past mistakes that even the most ardent critic will develop a warm respect for you.

MARTIN LUTHER KING JR. (1929–68),
Spingarn Medal, 1957; civil rights leader

The NAACP and other civil rights groups rally
at the state capital in Florida to urge that all votes be counted in the
2000 presidential election.

(Photo by Robert King/Newsmakers)

6

———❖———

GAINING POLITICAL POWER

Those of us who speak out are moved by a deep sense
of the fragility of our self-worth. It is the determination to protect our sense of who we are that leads us to
risk criticism, alienation, and serious loss while most
others similarly harmed, remain silent.

DERRICK BELL. member; law professor

Although the NAACP does not become involved in par-
tisan politics, the organization has, from its inception,
worked diligently to affect government policies that impact
African-Americans.

Their Washington bureau represents one of the primary
forces lobbying for civil rights in the nation's capital. In 1928
the NAACP participated in four court cases to enforce black
voting rights and in 1930 successfully fought President
Herbert Hoover's appointment of a North Carolina judge to
the Supreme Court. The judge had endorsed an amendment
to his state constitution approving a poll tax and a literacy

test for voters, tactics used most often to prevent blacks from voting.

Politicians and elected officials have long understood the potential power of black votes, and the disfranchisement of African-Americans, particularly in the South, was a pivotal issue for the NAACP. Medgar Evers, field secretary in Mississippi, was assassinated in 1963 largely because he was registering black voters. The NAACP lobbied hard for the Voting Rights Bill signed by President Lyndon Johnson in 1965. That bill enfranchised hundreds of thousands of blacks in the South. Soon thereafter, blacks were elected to offices for the first time since Reconstruction, a hundred years earlier. Recognizing this voting power, President Jimmy Carter appointed more blacks (and women and Hispanics) to federal courts than all the previous administrations combined.

Evidence that enfranchising black voters remains an issue came in June 2000 when the Harrisburg, Pennsylvania, branch of the NAACP led the fight to strike down a thirty-five-year-old law prohibiting those behind bars and ex-felons from voting. Judge Joseph T. Doyle rescinded the law one week prior to the state's deadline to register new voters. The NAACP has also targeted twenty-two other states whose laws prohibit voter participation by ex-felons.

In January 2001 the NAACP joined other organizations in filing a historic lawsuit to eliminate discriminatory and unequal voting policies and practices from Florida's electoral system. Kweisi Mfume, president and CEO, said, "There was evidence of massive voter disfranchisement of people of color during the [2000] presidential election. The election in Florida was conducted in a manner which was unfair, illegal, immoral, and undemocratic."

Let me now say to every Negro in the country: You must register. You must vote. And you must learn, so your choice advances your interests and the interests of the nation.

LYNDON B. JOHNSON,
president of the United States, 1963–69
(signing the Voting Rights Act, 1965)

ORGANIZING POWER

A people who can manage [twenty generations of slavery and five generations of racist oppression] and still give the world blood plasma, jazz, and Dennis Rodman are a force to be reckoned with.

JUDY DOTHARD SIMMONS.
contributing editor, *The Crisis*

—◦—

Malcolm is gone and Martin is gone, and it is up to all of us to nourish the hope they gave us.

LENA HORNE. Spingarn Medal, 1983;
vocalist, actress

If we can finally succeed in translating the idea of leadership into that of service, we may soon find it possible to lift the Negro to a higher level. Under leadership we have come to the ghetto; by service within the ranks, we may work our way out of it.

CARTER G. WOODSON (1875–1950),
Spingarn Medal, 1926; historian, educator,
founder of Negro History Week

Community service that stops short of community organizing will always be insufficient.

CLAYBORNE CARSON, member; director and
senior editor of the Martin Luther King Jr. Papers
Project, Stanford University

Salvation for the Negro must come from within. Our friends may help us. They cannot save us.

A. PHILIP RANDOLPH (1889–1979),
Spingarn Medal, 1942; founder of Brotherhood of
Sleeping Car Porters international union

The thinking colored people of the United States must stop being stampeded by the word *segregation*. It is the race conscious black man cooperating together in his own institutions and movements who will eventually emancipate the colored race.

W. E. B. DuBois (1868–1963), founder;
Crisis editor, 1910–34; Spingarn Medal, 1920

In order to take a stand, we must raise our standard from style to substance.

JAMAL-HARRISON BRYANT, former youth director; founder and pastor, Empowerment Temple AME, Baltimore

———◆———

You cannot liberate yourself by learning the oppressor's language because all the things that oppress you are built into the linguistic environment.

AUGUST WILSON, Theater Award, 1992; author of *Two Trains Running, Fences,* and other plays

I won't put my life in the hands of fate or in the hands of anyone who doesn't know me.

ANITA BAKER. Image Award, 1990;
vocalist and philanthropist

———◆———

[The Mississippi Freedom Democratic Party was] so naive. We didn't realize that the great liberals of our times, such as [Senator Paul] Douglas, Hubert Humphrey, and Lyndon Johnson, talked more about principles than they lived by them. . . . This was one reason why they got elected to office.

AARON HENRY (1922–1997),
founder, Coahoma County, Mississippi, branch, 1953;
state president, 1960–94; state legislator, 1979–95

The reason we need affirmative action is because we've had so much negative action . . . beginning with slavery and continuing with African-Americans being treated as second-class citizens for more than two centuries.

MARY FRANCES BERRY, member; chair,
U.S. Commission on Civil Rights;
author and history professor

⸺◆⸺

After all, democracy takes place when the silenced find a voice, and when we begin to listen to what they have to say.

LANI GUINIER, Legal Defense and Educational
Fund, 1981–89; law professor

To speak out provoke[s] violence; to remain silent encourage[s] death. It [is] a dilemma not at all new to people of color, or women.

ALICE WALKER. Image Award 1986; author of *The Color Purple, The Way Forward Is With a Broken Heart*, and other books

———•———

We will remember not the words of our enemies but the silence of our friends.

MARTIN LUTHER KING JR. (1929–68), Spingarn Medal, 1957; civil rights leader

WIELDING POWER

It's about performance. Results are what count. We must demand, and deliver, the best from ourselves. . . . Our fate in the long run has never rested with who is in the White House.

EARL G. GRAVES. Spingarn Medal, 1999;
publisher, *Black Enterprise* magazine

———◆———

We need . . . those positions that are gatekeepers. [Gatekeepers] decide what is on the front page and what gets buried in the back pages.

SPIKE (SHELTON) LEE. Image Award, 1994;
filmmaker, director, actor

It is especially heartening to me to see the active and often heroic part that leading Negro artists—singers, actors, writers, comedians, musicians—are playing today in the freedom struggle. . . . The Negro artist . . . has every right to be "controversial."

PAUL ROBESON (1898–1976),
Spingarn Medal, 1945; singer, actor, activist

———•———

[Voting] makes a difference because it reflects our interests and calls attention to our needs.

HAZEL DUKES, president, New York state
conference; former national president

A "winner-takes-all" culture suppresses voter participation. It reduces politics to a game in which voters become spectators rather than active citizens. . . . Where everyone can win something, genuine collaboration is possible.

LANI GUINIER, Legal Defense and Educational
Fund, 1981–89; law professor

When poor people feel they make a difference, they vote. There's no apathy; there's disappointment.

DOROTHY TILLMAN, member;
Chicago alderwoman

On voting day, [the black church] can't just pray. We get vans and buses and get people to the polls.

JULIUS C. HOPE, national director,
Religious Affairs Department;
pastor, New Grace Baptist Church, Detroit

———

Black people have done wonderful things for this country (saved its soul, in fact), and we have been an example to the world in the process. . . . If we did so much when we had so little, think of what we can do now that we have so much more.

VERNON JORDAN, Springarn Medal, 2001;
lawyer, businessman, Washington, D.C.

Only when blacks become politically independent can they make either party responsive to their demands and needs.

ARCHIBALD GRIMKÉ (1849–1930), founder;
president, Washington, D.C., branch, 1913–24;
diplomat and author; Spingarn Medal, 1919

———◆———

The ballot, while no longer conceived of as a magic key, is recognized as the indispensable weapon in a persistent fight for full citizenship . . . a tool to be used in the ultimate demolition of the whole outmoded structure of Jim Crow.

HENRY LEE MOON (1901–85),
Crisis editor, 1967–74

It takes an unusual politician to have respect for any man who is not in position to help him get in or stay in office.

BENJAMIN E. MAYS (1895–1984),
Spingarn Medal, 1982;
president, Morehouse College, Atlanta

———◆———

We must hold all newly elected and incumbent officeholders responsible for their actions—and remind them that the votes they cast will be remembered next Election Day. They cannot celebrate Dr. [Martin Luther] King's birthday in January and vote to destroy his dream the rest of the year.

JULIAN BOND, board chair since 1998; president, Atlanta branch, 1973–87; former Georgia legislator; civil rights professor

If you live in an oppressive society, you've got to be very resilient. You can't let each little thing crush you. You have to take every encounter and make yourself larger, rather than allow yourself to be diminished by it.

JAMES EARL JONES,
Image Award Hall of Fame, 1990; actor

———————

I don't think you can bring the races together by talking about the differences between them. I'd rather talk about the similarities, about what's universal in their experiences.

BILL (WILLIAM H.) COSBY JR.,
Spingarn Medal, 1985; comedian, actor,
philanthropist, educator

I always felt that if a white person did not understand what was going on with black people and how we were treated and humiliated almost every day, then they were not friends of mine, at all.

> OSCAR ROBERTSON, board of trustees;
> businessman and Hall of Fame basketball player

———◆———

What you have to do—white or black—you have to recognize that you have certain feelings about the other race, good or bad. And then get rid of 'em. But you can't get rid of them until you recognize them.

> THURGOOD MARSHALL (1908–93), director,
> Legal Defense and Educational Fund, 1936–61;
> Spingarn Medal, 1946;
> U.S. Supreme Court justice, 1967–91

The only way to waste your vote is not to use it. The propaganda that "a vote for Nader is . . . a wasted vote" is just that—propaganda to keep us enslaved to a two-party system with a one-party mind-set.

JUDY DOTHARD SIMMONS,

contributing editor, *Crisis*

———————

[It would be] infinitely better for us to throw our votes away upon a great man who stands for real democracy than to shame ourselves, our people, our country.

W. E. B. DU BOIS (1868–1963), founder;

Crisis editor, 1910–34; Spingarn Medal, 1920

Through the struggle and victory, Negroes tested their own strength and won. They learned unmistakably that they possess irresistible power if they become conscious of it and unite.

DAISY BATES (1914–99), Spingarn Medal
(with the Little Rock Nine), 1958;
state president, Arkansas;
journalist

———•———

Many millions of white families, as well as others, have benefited from [Thurgood] Marshall's crusade to deliver justice in the courtroom to the most vulnerable people in America.

CARL T. ROWAN (1925–2000),
Spingarn Medal, 1997;
author, syndicated columnist

Being a lawyer means not only sharing the pain of other people's suffering, but also accepting the burden of their trust.

JOHNNIE L. COCHRAN JR., member;
attorney at law

Discrimination is more subtle today. Thurgood Marshall, Charles Houston, and other leaders dismantled the doctrine of legally enforced segregation. . . . As the LDF moves into the twenty-first century, I hope to help make these protections a reality.

ELAINE R. JONES, director-counsel since 1993,
Legal Defense and Educational Fund (LDF)

Florida and Texas each disfranchise more than six hundred thousand people as ex-felons. . . . Taxation without representation is unfair based on the American principles of justice and freedom.

EDYTHE FLEMINGS HALL, branch president, Prince George's County, Maryland; member of the national board since 1998; minority business enterprise consultant

———◆—◆———

We can no longer allow politicians to come around at election time and kiss our babies but not [support] after-school programs and prenatal care.

JAMAL-HARRISON BRYANT, former youth director; founder and pastor, Empowerment Temple AME, Baltimore

We must be ready, willing, and able to raise our voices and wield our influence at all levels of political representation, from our local school boards to city hall to the state house.

EARL G. GRAVES. Spingarn Medal, 1999; publisher, *Black Enterprise* magazine

Mary Church Terrell, W. E. B. DuBois, and Arthur Springarn,
three of the NAACP's founders and charter members

*(Library of Congress, Prints & Photographs Division,
Visual Materials from the NAACP records)*

7

A BRIEF HISTORY
OF THE NAACP

We want anybody and everybody in this organization
who shares our values and our goals, and we don't
have any color barriers to membership.

JULIAN BOND, board chair since 1998;
president, Atlanta branch, 1973–87; former Georgia
legislator; civil rights professor

On the one hundredth anniversary of Abraham Lincoln's birth in 1909, Mary White Ovington, a social activist and descendant of abolitionists; William English Walling, a wealthy Southerner living in New York who wrote for the *Independent* newspaper; and Dr. Henry Moskowitz, a social worker, met to form an organization to right the nation's wrongs against the Negro.

With other white liberals in New York City, they established the National Negro Committee in response to a race riot the previous summer in Springfield, Illinois, Lincoln's hometown. In the riot, eight blacks were murdered and two

125

thousand others fled their homes and the town. Wealthy and influential newspaper publisher Oswald Garrison Villard, grandson of famed abolitionist William Lloyd Garrison, was a member of the committee and wrote a "call" that he printed in his paper, the *New York Evening Post*. The call asked "all believers in democracy to join in a national conference for the discussion of present evils, the voicing of protests, and the renewal of the struggle for civil and political liberty."

Among those signing the call were members of the Niagara Movement, which had been founded four years earlier by W. E. B. DuBois, a professor at Atlanta University; Ida B. Wells-Barnett, Chicago journalist and activist; William Monroe Trotter, publisher of the Boston *Guardian*, and other black leaders. Ovington had been corresponding with DuBois for some time and had attended the first Niagara Movement conference in 1906 as a reporter for Villard's newspaper.

In effect the committee absorbed the Niagara Movement and in 1910 adopted as their name the National Association for the Advancement of Colored People. They envisioned the organization as a forum for a full discussion of the conditions of black people in the United States and as a force for achieving the rights being denied African-Americans. Most of the original board members and officers were white; however, DuBois, as director of research and publicity and founding editor of the *Crisis*, the NAACP journal, was, in effect, their public voice and the top-ranking African-American in the organization at its inception.

Like any other large, successful organization, the NAACP has had its share of trials over the years, with differences in approaches to problems, personality clashes, the generation gap, maneuvering for power, and a sometimes diminished appreciation of the efforts of its female members. Yet, the NAACP always manages to work its way through these conflicts and to continue its pursuit of the mission for which it was founded.

The quotations included below highlight some of the issues the NAACP has wrestled with throughout its history and feature several of the people who have been pivotal figures in that history.

There is a great prejudice against the colored people. . . . It will take one hundred years to eradicate this prejudice, and we must deal with it as practical men. Segregation is not humiliating but a benefit, and ought to be so regarded by you gentlemen.

WOODROW WILSON,
president of the United States, 1913–21
(to NAACP leaders in 1914 after his decision to segregate the entire workforce of the federal government)

EARLY YEARS

We will not be satisfied to take . . . less than our full manhood rights . . . and until we get these rights we will never cease to protest and assail the ears of America. . . . Lest this, our common fatherland . . . become in truth the land of the Thief and the home of the Slave.

W. E. B. DuBois (1868–1963), founder;
Crisis editor, 1910–34; Spingarn Medal, 1920
(from the Niagara Movement Resolutions at
Harpers Ferry, 1906)

———————

[The NAACP] was denounced as radical, revolutionary, subversive; . . . a "social equality" [whites and blacks socializing as equals] society. . . . [There are] a series of far-flung barriers against amalgamation of the two races; except so far as it may come about by white men with colored women.

JAMES WELDON JOHNSON (1871–1938),
field secretary, 1916–19; chief officer, 1920–30;
wrote lyrics for "Lift Every Voice and Sing"

By some I was severely criticized because I joined the NAACP because it was supposed to have been founded to counteract the influence of Booker T. Washington and to discredit him. . . . I was a charter member . . . [and] traveled a thousand miles to attend its first meeting in New York City.

MARY CHURCH TERRELL (1863–1954),
vice president, Washington, D.C., branch;
lecturer, clubwoman, activist

Oswald Garrison Villard, vice president of the board of the NAACP . . . was white, a latter-day abolitionist . . . [and] a little overeager to dispense solutions for all Negro problems, a failing common to many good-hearted white liberals.

ROY WILKINS (1901–81),
executive director, 1955–77;
Spingarn Medal, 1964

[W. E. B.] DuBois conducted himself in public like a wary lion, concealing uncertainty and sensitivity behind a proud tread and a readiness to spring at the first shadow in his path.

DAVID LEVERING LEWIS. professor, author, and
W. E. B. DuBois biographer

—————

Those founding white liberals [of the NAACP] had . . . one rather embarrassing problem: while the new NAACP was long on conscience, it was very short on contacts with Negroes.

ROY WILKINS (1901–1981)
executive director, 1955–1977;
Spingarn Medal, 1964

The NAACP . . . has fallen short of the expectations of its founders. The reason is not far to seek. It has kept Miss Mary White Ovington as chairman of the executive committee. Miss Ovington's heart is in this work, but her experience has been confined solely to . . . a few minor incidents along the color line.

IDA B. WELLS-BARNETT (1862–1931),
founder; newspaper publisher and journalist,
antilynching crusader

———•———

[Mary White Ovington] was no fair-weather friend. . . . She shared the problems of the race from days when it was almost a crime for white people to associate with colored people.

CARL MURPHY (1889–1967),
Spingarn Medal, 1955; board member;
editor, publisher, *Baltimore Afro-American*

Something is wrong when patriotic, loyal citizens ready and able to fight, are compelled to petition their government for an unprescribed approval to fight for it.

ROBERT SENGSTACKE ABBOTT (1868–1940),
member; publisher and founder, *The Chicago Defender*
(at a May 1917 NAACP meeting, after the
United States had entered World War I)

The first Mississippi branch [of the NAACP] was started in 1918. . . . Being a member meant putting one's life on the line.

MYRLIE EVERS-WILLIAMS. board chair,
1995–98; Spingarn Medal, 1998

The work of the next decade will have to be concentrated in the South.

CHARLES HAMILTON HOUSTON (1895–1950),
Spingarn Medal, 1950; chief legal counsel, 1935–38;
law professor (1934 letter to Walter White)

———

I came to the Association because I felt that I could make a contribution to the struggle for human justice and equality.

ELLA BAKER (1903–86),
assistant field secretary, 1941–43;
director of branches, 1943–46

Black women are the backbone of every institution, but sometimes they are not recognized as even being there, even in the civil rights movement.

DOROTHY I. HEIGHT. Spingarn Medal, 1993; former CEO, National Council of Negro Women

———◆———

Would the [black] struggle have come this far without the indomitable determination of its women?

PAULI MURRAY (1910–85), member; educator, attorney, and Episcopal priest

Years later, Stokely Carmichael, H. Rap Brown, and company would cut [disrespect] me much as I had cut DuBois [in 1923]. Times change; the souls of young men and old men don't seem to.

ROY WILKINS (1901–81),
executive director, 1955–77;
Spingarn Medal, 1964

———◆———

The NAACP helped black teachers in many parts of the South fight for equal salaries . . . . In Birmingham . . . there were a lot of delays [but] the NAACP and the teachers finally won, and pay equality started in the fall of 1945.

ROSA PARKS. Spingarn Medal, 1979;
branch secretary, Montgomery, Alabama, 1943–57;
founder, Rosa and Raymond Parks
Institute for Self-Development

CIVIL RIGHTS MOVEMENT

Before there was an Equal Employment Opportunity Commission, or even a civil rights division of the Justice Department, there was just Thurgood [Marshall]. Black people ... from all over the country who had grievances but no recourse would call Thurgood.

ROGER WILKINS, chairman, *The New Crisis* Publishing Company, history professor

———

[In the 1950s] if a Negro joined the NAACP, his boss fired him. If he was a farmer, he lost his crop loan at planting time. If he rented land, his rent went up. If he owned, the bank foreclosed. Stores cut off his credit.

CHARLES EVERS, field secretary, Mississippi, 1963–69; former mayor, Fayette, Mississippi

It wasn't until after the 1954 [U.S.] Supreme Court decision that Mississippi school boards began seriously checking employees for NAACP membership.

AARON HENRY (1922–97), founder, Coahoma
County, Mississippi, branch, 1953;
state president, 1960–94; state legislator, 1979–95

———

Anyone who was against segregation was considered a Communist.

SEPTIMA CLARK (1898–1987),
fired by the Charleston, South Carolina,
board of education in 1956 for being a member of the
NAACP; educational leader

The [U.S.] Supreme Court decisions of 1954 to 1964 are exceptional . . . In one case after the other, segregation was stricken as unconstitutional. This resulted in a revolution in this country—a social revolution.

CONSTANCE BAKER MOTLEY. Legal Defense
and Educational Fund, 1946–64; federal judge

———

The schools will be integrated. Negroes will hold government jobs, they will work in industry on an equal basis, and all theaters will be integrated.

KELLY ALEXANDER SR. (1915–85),
board member, 1950–85; chairman, 1984–85
(Charlotte, North Carolina, 1962)

The most famous initials in America are the NAACP. The most written about voluntary association in America is the NAACP. The most damned [by others] group of citizens is the NAACP.

LANGSTON HUGHES (1902–67),
Spingarn Medal, 1960; poet and author

———•———

In Mississippi, the [civil rights] movement families were all NAACP families.

ROBERT PARRIS MOSES, organizer, Mississippi Freedom Democratic Party and 1964 Freedom Summer Project; founder, Algebra Project

Because of the absence of [federal registrars as provided in the Voting Rights Act] we must canvass for voters on back roads in the middle of the night and take our chances.

FANNIE LOU HAMER (1917–77), civil rights
leader; founder, Mississippi Freedom Democratic Party
(in Sunflower County, home of U.S. senator
James Eastland, 1965)

All the sixties did, in reality, was save the political entity we know as the United States from self-destruction.

NIKKI GIOVANNI. Image Award, 1997;
poet and professor

When I took over this organization, I had plans for expanding the mission of the NAACP. I had no idea I would be fighting to retain what I thought we had already won.

BENJAMIN L. HOOKS,
executive director, 1977–93; Baptist minister, lawyer,
and former member of the Federal Communications
Commission (his tenure at the NAACP coincided with
the administration of President Ronald Reagan)

———◆———

Marching On

The NAACP's strengths are its people . . . .most importantly—and most often overlooked is the structure of twenty-two hundred branches scattered all across the country and in several foreign countries. . . . It is those people who, after work, after school . . . do the work of the NAACP. . . . That is our overwhelming strength and always has been.

JULIAN BOND, board chair since 1998; president, Atlanta branch, 1973–87; former Georgia legislator; civil rights professor

---

Merely because you don't need the NAACP this minute doesn't mean you might not one day.

RALPH WILEY, member; author of *Why Black People Tend to Shout* and other books

[The NAACP] is willing to work cooperatively with prison administrators . . . [but] it will not allow racially discriminatory practices to go unchallenged.

LEROY MOBLEY, founder, Prison Program

———•———

The church is the communicative arm of the NAACP. We try to get the word out. TV isn't going to do it. Radio isn't. The church has to do it.

JULIUS C. HOPE, national director,
Religious Affairs Department;
pastor, New Grace Baptist Church, Detroit

I don't know for sure that [the NAACP] is out of touch with young black Americans. But I know they don't hear us well.

BOWYER G. FREEMAN. branch president,
Howard County, Maryland

———◆———

My leadership style is one to help organize, empower, and mobilize people at the grassroots level.

BENJAMIN CHAVIS. executive secretary, 1993–94
(accepting his new position as chief officer, at forty-five
the youngest ever, resigned in the wake of a scandal)

I have given my entire life to [the NAACP]. I will not see it destroyed.

ENOLIA MCMILLAN, national president,
1984–87; branch president, Baltimore, 1969–84
(at the Annual Meeting, 1995)

———◆———

This is an American institution, and it can become the premier organization it once was.

A. LEON HIGGINBOTHAM (1928–98),
member, national board; Spingarn Medal, 1996;
chief justice, U.S. Court of Appeals
(to Kweisi Mfume during search for new CEO)

———◆———

I think that the brother has his hands full . . . but if anybody can do it, Kweisi Mfume is the right man for the job.

WENDELL ANTHONY, branch president, Detroit;
pastor of Fellowship Chapel, Detroit

I hope that we do not lose sight of the hard work of those who care about the NAACP; that we have almost a miracle in being able to keep the doors open [in the last ten months].

MYRLIE EVERS-WILLIAMS,
board chair, 1995–98; Spingarn Medal, 1998
(announcing the selection of Mfume as
new president and CEO, December 1995)

———◆———

The NAACP has reclaimed its position as America's premier civil rights organization. In a December 2000 poll, the NAACP enjoyed a favorable rating of 84 percent from black respondents.

JULIAN BOND, board chair since 1998; president,
Atlanta branch, 1973–87; former Georgia legislator;
civil rights professor

My election shows that the NAACP is creating space for the next generation to step into meaningful leadership positions. There has always been a place for young people in the NAACP and this is further evidence of it.

ROSLYN MCCALLISTER BROCK,
board member since 1985, vice chair since 2001;
director of business and community development
for a Baltimore health organization

———

Broadening its traditional definition of itself is the next evolutionary step for the NAACP and must be a top priority.

KWEISI MFUME, president and CEO since 1996;
represented Baltimore in U.S. Congress, 1986–96

CHRONOLOGY OF
NAACP LANDMARKS

⸺◈⸺

1905   W. E. B. DuBois and twenty-nine other blacks (including William Monroe Trotter and Ida D. Wells Barnett) form the Niagara Movement "to claim every single right that belongs to a freeborn American."

1909   National Negro Conference held by a group of liberal whites and philanthropists including Oswald Garrison Villard and Mary White Ovington. Absorbs most of the membership of the Niagara Movement and forms the National Association for the Advancement of Colored People.

1910   DuBois establishes and becomes editor of the *Crisis*, the association's official journal.

1911   New York City branch established.

1912   Detroit branch receives charter. Branches opened in Baltimore, Boston, and Chicago.

1914   Spingarn Medal designed by Joel E. Spingarn,

treasurer and later president, to stimulate distinguished achievement by Negroes and to call the attention of the world to such achievement. Awarded annually.

Los Angeles branch founded in the home of Drs. John and Vada Somerville.

1915   Victory in *Guinn v. the U.S.* when U.S. Supreme Court strikes down grandfather clause used to prevent blacks from voting.

1916   Joel Spingarn prevails on the secretary of war to set up a segregated camp in Des Moines, Iowa, to train Negro officers for the U.S. army.

1917   Organized silent march down Fifth Avenue in New York City to protest the massacre of blacks in East St. Louis, Illinois, and to insist that America be made safe for democracy.

1919   *Thirty Years of Lynching in the United States* published.

Two hundred twenty branches; 56,345 members on tenth anniversary.

1920   James Weldon Johnson becomes first black executive secretary.

1927   Victory in *Nixon v. Herndon,* U.S. Supreme Court, for rights of blacks to participate in Democratic Party elections.

1930   Walter White becomes executive secretary.

1934   After a series of disagreements with White, DuBois resigns and returns to Atlanta University.

1935   Louis T. Wright, M.D., becomes first black board chairman.

1936   Legal Defense and Educational Fund established with Thurgood Marshall as director.

1941   Executive Order 8802 issued by President Franklin D. Roosevelt, banning discrimination in industries holding government contracts for war production and in the training for jobs in war industries.

1942   Washington bureau established to lobby Congress on issues of equality for African-Americans.

1944   DuBois returns as director of special research.

1945   W. E. B. DuBois and Walter White represent the NAACP as consultants at the founding meeting of the United Nations.

1947   Harry S. Truman attends NAACP convention, the first U.S. president to do so.

1948   President Truman issues Executive Orders abolishing discrimination in the federal civil service and in the armed forces.

        DuBois's contract is not renewed and he retires from the NAACP at age eighty.

After a thirty-one-year fight, the U.S. Supreme Court in a unanimous decision outlaws restrictive covenants (clauses forbidding the sale of property to a buyer because of his race) in real estate deeds in *Shelley v. Kraemer.*

1954   Victory in *Brown v. Board of Education:* unanimous decision banning segregation in public schools handed down by U.S. Supreme Court.

1955   Roy Wilkins becomes executive secretary.

Rosa Parks, secretary of the Montgomery branch, refuses to give her seat to a white rider, thus sparking the Montgomery bus boycott.

1956   U.S. Supreme Court rules segregated seating on public conveyances unconstitutional for a victorious end to the Montgomery bus boycott organized by E. D. Nixon, past branch president.

Detroit branch holds first Freedom Fund Dinner.

1957   Nine students, led by Arkansas state president Daisy Bates and escorted by federal troops, desegregate Central High School in Little Rock.

NAACP Legal Defense and Educational Fund becomes separate organization.

1960   Four members of the youth division begin the sit-in movement in Greensboro, North Carolina.

1963　Participation in March on Washington demanding end to discrimination in housing, education, and employment (August 28).

W. E. B. DuBois dies in Ghana (August 27).

1964　U.S. Supreme Court orders Alabama to permit the NAACP to resume operations that had been banned in the state since 1956.

1965　Voting Rights Bill passed as result of lobbying by Washington bureau and other efforts.

1966　Constance Baker Motley, former NAACP attorney, becomes first black woman appointed as a federal judge.

1967　Thurgood Marshall, former NAACP attorney, becomes first black appointed to U.S. Supreme Court.

Image Awards established by Beverly Hills/Hollywood branch to recognize excellence and positive images of African-Americans in the performing arts—theater, film, television, athletics.

1972　Prison Program, founded by Leroy Mobley, receives charter.

1977　Benjamin Hooks succeeds Wilkins as executive director.

ACT-SO (Afro Academic, Cultural, Technological and Scientific Olympics) established. Program to recognize academic excellence of young people created by Vernon Jarrett.

1980 NAACP participates with other groups in the first National Conference for a Black Agenda.

1983 Margaret Bush Wilson, board chair, suspends Benjamin Hooks, executive director; ten days later Wilson stripped of her power by majority vote of the board.

1986 National headquarters moved from New York City to Baltimore.

First telecast of Image Awards.

1987 Beverly Hills/Hollywood branch separates Theater Awards from other Image Awards.

1991 Massive project to redraw district lines helps to increase minority representation in Congress.

Thurgood Marshall retires from U.S. Supreme Court.

Image Awards moved from Beverly Hills/Hollywood branch to national office.

1992 NationsBank commits $10 billion to establish resource centers run by the NAACP to advise African-Americans on small-business loans, mortgages, and other financial matters.

First telecast of ACT-SO competition.

1993 Benjamin Chavis succeeds Hooks as executive director.

1994   Chavis resigns under pressure.

1996   Kweisi Mfume leaves U.S. Congress to become president and CEO.

2000   Agreements signed with television networks for a series of initiatives to increase opportunities for people of color in the industry.

2001   Lawsuit filed, in conjunction with other organizations, in Florida to eliminate discriminatory and unequal voting policies and practices from Florida's electoral system.

Eleanor Roosevelt presents the 1939 Spingarn Medal
to Marian Anderson.

(Library of Congress, Prints & Photographs Division,

Visual Materials from the NAACP records)

Spingarn Medal Winners

The Spingarn Medal was created in 1914 by Joel E. Spingarn, then chairman of the NAACP Board of Directors. Spingarn designed a gold medal to be awarded annually to an American of African descent for the highest or noblest achievement of the preceding year or years. The purpose of the award is to stimulate achievement by African-Americans, to call the attention of the world to such achievement, and to stimulate the ambition of black youth. It is the NAACP's most distinguished award. In his will, Spingarn left a fund to continue the award "to perpetuate the lifelong interest of my brother, Arthur B. Spingarn, and of myself in the achievement of the American Negro."

Henry Louis (Hank) Aaron, baseball player, *in recognition of his singular home-run record achievement,* 1975

Alvin Ailey, dancer and choreographer, *in recognition of his international eminence in the field of dance,* 1976

Marian Anderson, concert singer, *for her special achievement in the field of music,* 1939

Maya Angelou, author, poet, actress, playwright, director, *in praise of her passionate autobiographical pursuit of truth and integrity,* 1994

Daisy Bates and the Little Rock Nine, *for their role in upholding the basic ideals of American democracy in the face of continuing harassment and constant threats of bodily injury,* 1958

Mary McLeod Bethune, founder, president, Bethune-Cookman College, *for establishing and building up Bethune-Cookman and for speaking out against injustice in the South as well as the North without compromise or fear,* 1935

Tom Bradley, mayor of Los Angeles, *in salutation to a lifetime of growth and achievement,* 1984

William Stanley Braithwaite, poet and literary critic, *for distinguished achievement in literature,* 1918

Edward W. Brooke, III, Republican senator from Massachusetts, *for being the first black to win popular election to the U.S. Senate,* 1967

Ralph J. Bunche, diplomat, *for his contribution to the settlement of armed conflict in the Middle East,* 1949

Harry T. Burleigh, composer, pianist, singer, *for excellence in the field of creative music,* 1917

George Washington Carver, head of Research Department and director of the Experiment Station at Tuskegee Institute, *for research in agricultural chemistry*, 1923

Charles W. Chesnutt, author, *for his pioneer work as a literary artist and his long career as scholar, worker, and freeman*, 1928

Kenneth B. Clark, professor of psychology, College of the City of New York, *for his research that contributed significantly to the Supreme Court decision banning segregation in public education*, 1961

William H. "Bill" Cosby Jr., comedian, actor, *for his spectacular career and leadership through personal example*, 1985

Sammy Davis Jr., dancer, singer, actor, *for his talent and his commitment to justice, freedom, equality, and the brotherhood of all mankind*, 1968

Charles R. Drew, scientist, *for his research on blood plasma that led to the establishment of a blood plasma bank that served as a model for the American Red Cross blood banks*, 1944

William E. B. DuBois, author and editor of *The Crisis*, *for founding and calling the Pan-African Congress*, 1920

Edward Kennedy (Duke) Ellington, composer and orchestra leader, *for his outstanding musical achievements*, 1959

Medgar Wiley Evers, NAACP field secretary for Mississippi, *for his courage, dedication, and martyrdom in the fight for freedom*, presented posthumously, 1963

Myrlie Evers-Williams, civil rights activist, *in gratitude for winning the NAACP chairmanship during its deepest crisis and leading the Association from a severe deficit to its first budget surplus in five years,* 1998

John Hope Franklin, historian, author, educator, *in recognition of an unrelenting quest for truth to establish a new standard in reportage of American history on a racially inclusive basis,* 1995

Charles S. Gilpin, actor, *for his performance in the title role of the play* The Emperor Jones, *1921*

Earl G. Graves, entrepreneur, publisher, civic leader, *with gratitude for an unflagging commitment to justice, equality, and excellence in the pursuit of the American dream, 1999*

Archibald H. Grimké, U.S. consul in Santo Domingo; founder and president, Washington, D.C., branch, *for seventy years of distinguished service to his race and country, 1919*

Alexander Palmer (Alex) Haley, author, lecturer, *for his unsurpassed effectiveness in portraying the legendary story of an American of African descent, 1977*

Richard Berry Harrison, actor, *for years of work as dramatic reader and entertainer for the mass of colored people in church and school, 1931*

William H. Hastie, jurist and educator, *for his distinguished career as a jurist and uncompromising championship of equal justice, 1943*

Roland Hayes, singer, *for the artistry through which he interpreted the beauty of the Negro folk song and won a place as soloist with the Boston Symphony Orchestra, 1924*

Dorothy I. Height, National Council of Negro Women, *in recognition of six decades of leadership in the struggle for equity and human rights for all people, 1993*

A. Leon Higginbotham, jurist, scholar, educator, *in recognition of his consistently passionate pursuit of justice and equality under law, 1996*

Benjamin L. Hooks, executive director, NAACP, *in recognition of a superlative career as a lawyer, minister, jurist, scholar, orator, national public servant, 1986*

John Hope, president, Atlanta University, *for being a distinguished leader of his race, presented posthumously, 1936*

Lena Horne, vocalist, actress, *in recognition of her distinguished career and unfaltering dedication and commitment to the principles of equality and justice, 1983*

Charles Hamilton Houston, chairman, NAACP Legal Committee, *for leadership in the legal profession and inspired teaching of youth, presented posthumously, 1950*

Langston Hughes, poet, author, and playwright, *for being a major American writer, considered by many the Poet Laureate of the Negro race, 1960*

Henry A. Hunt, principal, Ft. Valley High & Industrial School, *for twenty-five years of faithful and devoted service in the education of Negroes in rural Georgia, 1930*

Jesse Jackson, clergyman, political and civil rights leader, *in recognition of the stature he has attained as a national leader in the political arena winning 7 million votes in the 1988 Democratic Primary Election, 1989*

James Weldon Johnson, U.S. consul in Venezuela and Nicaragua; national secretary NAACP, *for distinguished achievement as author, diplomat, and public servant, 1925*

John H. Johnson, founder and CEO, Johnson Publishing Company, *for his ingenuity and enterprise in publishing and contributions to the enhancement of the Negro's self-image, 1966*

Mordecai Wyatt Johnson, president, Howard University, *for successful administration as Howard's first Negro president, especially securing U.S. government appropriations, 1929*

Barbara Jordan, lawyer, educator, political leader, *in recognition of her historical achievements in Texas politics and for her unyielding belief in the equality of all humans, 1992*

Vernon Jordan, lawyer, presidential adviser, *for his decades of untiring efforts to ensure that African-Americans are identified as people of dignity and respect, 2001*

Percy L. Julian, research chemist, *for his many important discoveries that have saved countless lives, 1947*

Ernest E. Just, professor, Howard University, *for research in biology, 1915*

Damon J. Keith, jurist, *in tribute to his defense of constitutional principles as revealed in a series of memorable decisions handed down as a U.S. District Court judge, 1974*

Martin Luther King Jr., civil rights leader, *for his creative contributions to the fight for freedom and leadership role in the Montgomery bus boycott, 1957*

Theodore K. Lawless, physician, educator, and philanthropist, *for his research and experiments which have enlarged the area of scientific knowledge in dermatology, 1954*

Jacob Lawrence, artist, *for the success with which he has turned his artistic gifts and values to the portrayal of Negro life and history, 1970*

Rayford W. Logan, educator, historian, author, *for his penetrating monographs on adverse conditions affecting the people of Africa and Haiti, 1980*

Thurgood Marshall, special counsel of the NAACP, *for his distinguished service as a lawyer before the U.S. Supreme Court, 1946*

Benjamin E. Mays, president of Morehouse College, 1940–68, *in recognition of his intellectual honesty and compelling integrity in all circumstances, 1982*

Clarence M. Mitchell Jr., director, NAACP Washington Bureau, *for his pivotal role in enactment of the Civil Rights Act of 1968, 1969*

Harry T. Moore, leader of the NAACP in Florida, *for his martyrdom as a result of his work to abolish segregation at the University of Florida and to expand voting for African-Americans, presented posthumously, 1952*

Robert Russa Moton, president, Tuskegee Institute, *for his leadership as shown in the U.S. Veterans Hospital controversy at Tuskegee and his support of equal opportunity for blacks in the American public school systems, 1932*

Carl Murphy, editor, publisher, *for his leadership in leveling invidious racial barriers in employment, education, and recreation, 1955*

Anthony Overton, president, Victory Life Insurance Company, *for his successful business career, 1927*

Gordon Parks, photographer, writer, filmmaker, composer, *in recognition of his unique creativity as exemplified by his outstanding achievements, 1972*

Rosa L. Parks, community activist, *in tribute to the quiet courage and determination exemplified on a bus in Montgomery, Alabama, December 1, 1955, when she refused to surrender her seat to a white male passenger, 1979*

Frederick Douglass Patterson, educator, doctor of veterinary medicine, *in salutation of his efforts in the establishment in 1943 of the United Negro College Fund, 1988*

Colin Powell, general, U.S. army, chairman, U.S. Joint Chiefs of Staff, *in recognition of an unprecedented career of achievement in the nation's military, 1991*

Leontyne Price, Metropolitan Opera star, *in recognition of her talent and in appreciation of her contributions to the continuing crusade for justice, 1965*

A. Philip Randolph, president of the Brotherhood of Sleeping Car Porters, *for his unparalleled record of leadership in labor organization and national affairs, 1942*

Wilson C. Riles, California superintendent of education, *in recognition of the stature he has attained as a national leader in the field of education, 1973*

Paul Robeson, concert singer and actor, for distinguished achievement in the theater and on the stage, 1945

Jack Roosevelt Robinson, baseball player and businessman, *for his pioneering role in opening up major league baseball and his civic consciousness, 1956*

Carl T. Rowan, journalist, public servant, *in special tribute to the founding and developing of "Project Excellence," the Merit Scholarship Program for black college-bound students, 1997*

Mabel Keaton Staupers, leader, National Association of Colored Graduate Nurses, *for the successful movement to integrate Negro nurses into American life as equals, 1951*

Leon Howard Sullivan, activist clergyman, *in recognition of the inspiration and resourcefulness with which he has transmuted the social gospel into economic progress for his people, 1971*

Percy E. Sutton, businessman, community leader, *in recognition of his successes as lawyer, public official, pioneering businessman, 1987*

Mary B. Talbert, president, National Association of Colored Women, *for services to women and the restoration of the Frederick Douglass home, 1922*

Channing H. Tobias, *for his consistent role as a defender of fundamental American liberties, 1948*

Robert C. Weaver, administrator, Housing and Home Finance Agency, *for his advocacy of open occupany in housing and militant leadership in the struggle for human rights, 1962*

Walter White, executive secretary of the NAACP, *for his personal investigation of forty-one lynchings and eight race riots, 1937*

L. Douglas Wilder, governor, attorney, *in tribute to an extraordinary life of accomplishment, a grandson of slaves who has become governor of Virginia, 1990*

Roy Wilkins, executive director, NAACP, *for the militancy of his leadership, and the integrity of his performance, 1964*

Paul R. Williams, architect, *for his pioneering work as a creative designer of modern dwellings, 1953*

William Taylor Burwell Williams, dean of Tuskegee Institute, *for long service as field agent of the Slater and Jeanes Funds and the General Education Board, 1934*

Oprah Winfrey, businesswoman, actress, *for her exemplary leadership in helping people to become fully empowered, 2000*

Carter G. Woodson, author, historian, and founder of the Association *for the Study of Negro Life and History, for ten years' service collecting and publishing the records of blacks in America,* 1926

Louis T. Wright, surgeon, *for his contribution to healing and insisting on standards of excellence and equal opportunity for men and women in the field of medicine, 1940*

Richard Wright, author, *for his powerful depiction in his books of the effect of segregation and denial of opportunities on African-Americans, 1941*

Max Yergan, YMCA secretary in South Africa, *for his movement for interracial understanding among black and white students, 1933*

Andrew J. Young, U.S. ambassador to the United Nations, *for his major role in raising the consciousness of American citizens to the significance in world affairs of the massive African continent,* 1978

Charles Young, major, U.S. army, *for organizing the Liberian Constabulary and roads in the Republic of Liberia, West Africa,* 1916

Coleman A. Young, mayor of Detroit, *in recognition of his unparalleled record of affirmative action programs, crime reduction, improved police/community relations, and urban revitalization,* 1981

FURTHER READING

Aaron Henry: The Fire Ever Burning by Aaron Henry with Constance Curry, University Press of Mississippi, 2000.

Along This Way: The Autobiography of James Weldon Johnson, Da Capo Press, 1999.

A. Philip Randolph, Pioneer of the Civil Rights Movement by Paul F. Pfeffer, Louisiana State University Press, 1990.

Archibald Grimké: Portrait of a Black Independent by Dickson D. Bruce, Louisiana State University Press, 1993.

Balance of Power: The Negro Vote by Henry Lee Moon, Greenwood Publishing Group, 1977.

Black Enterprise Titans of the B.E. 100s: Black CEOs Who Redefined and Conquered American Business by Derek T. Dingle, John Wiley & Sons, 1999.

The Chicago NAACP and the Rise of Black Professional Leadership, 1910–1966 by Christopher Robert Reed, Indiana University Press, 1997.

A Colored Woman in a White World by Mary Church Terrell (African-American Women Writers Series, 1910–1940), G. K. Hall, 1996.

Crusade for Justice: The Autobiography of Ida B. Wells, edited by Alfreda Duster, University of Chicago Press, 1990.

Ella Baker: Freedom Bound by Joanne Grant, John Wiley & Sons, 1998.

From Slavery to Freedom: A History of African-Americans, 8th ed., by John Hope Franklin and Alfred A. Moss, Alfred A. Knopf, 2000.

Have No Fear: The Charles Evers Story by Charles Evers, John Wiley & Sons, 1997.

Inheritors of the Spirit: Mary White Ovington and the Founding of the NAACP by Carolyn Wedin, John Wiley & Sons, 1998.

In Search of Democracy: The NAACP Writings of James Weldon Johnson, Walter White, and Roy Wilkins, 1920–1977 by Sondra Kathryn Wilson, Oxford University Press, 1999.

Lift Every Voice and Sing: A Celebration of the Negro National Anthem, edited by Julian Bond and Sondra Kathryn Wilson, Random House, 2000.

Lift Every Voice: Turning a Civil Rights Setback into a New Vision of Social Justice by Lani Guinier, Simon & Schuster, 1998.

Lion in the Lobby: Clarence Mitchell Jr.'s Struggle for the Passage of Civil Rights Laws by Denton L. Watson, William Morrow and Company, 1990.

A Man Called White: The Autobiography of Walter White, The University of Georgia Press, 1995.

No Free Ride: From the Mean Streets to the Mainstream by Kweisi Mfume with Ron Stodghill II, Ballantine Books, 1996.

On Her Own Ground: The Life and Times of Madam C. J. Walker by A'Lelia Bundles, Scribner, 2001.

Stand Fast: The Autobiography of Roy Wilkins, Da Capo Press, 1994.

This Little Light of Mine: The Life of Fannie Lou Hamer by Kay Mills, Dutton, 1993.

Thurgood Marshall: American Revolutionary by Juan Williams, Times Books, Random House, 1998.

Watch Me Fly: What I Learned on the Way to Becoming the Woman I Was Meant to Be by Myrlie Evers-Williams, Little, Brown and Company, 1998.

W. E. B. DuBois: Biography of a Race, 1868–1919 by David Levering Lewis, Henry Holt, 1993.

W. E. B. DuBois: The Fight for Equality and the American Century, 1919–1963 by David Levering Lewis, Henry Holt, 2000.

When and Where We Enter: The Impact of Black Women on Race and Sex in America by Paula Giddings, William Morrow & Company, 1996.

NAACP PROGRAMS

ACT-SO

ACT-SO is an acronym for Afro Academic, Cultural, Technological and Scientific Olympics. This year-round enrichment program is designed to recruit, stimulate, improve, and encourage high academic and cultural achievement among African-American high school students. The twenty-four categories of competition are in the sciences, humanities, performing and visual arts. African-American high school students, enrolled in grades nine through twelve, who are citizens of the United States, who are amateurs in the categories of competition are eligible to compete in a local ACT-SO program to qualify for the national ACT-SO competition. Prizes consist of gold, silver, and bronze medals and cash scholarships. Community volunteers and business leaders serve as mentors, coaches, and judges.

For more information contact:
Rhonda K. Suttle, National Director
Phone: (410) 486-9160
E-mail: tsuttle@naacpnet.org

BACK TO SCHOOL/STAY IN SCHOOL

The theme of Back to School/Stay in School (BTS/SIS) is R.E.A.C.H. (Reaching Educational Achievement by Completing High School). The program is operated through the networking support of NAACP adult branches, college chapters, youth councils, churches, schools, community/civic organizations, and businesses.

For more information write or call:
NAACP Back to School/Stay in School Program
4805 Mt. Hope Drive
Baltimore, Maryland 21215
(410) 486-9144 and (410) 764-7357

DIVERSITY & HIGH-TECH CAREER FAIR

The NAACP Diversity & High-Tech Career Fair provides a productive forum for finding a new job with a company that values a diverse workforce. The career fairs are held periodically in locales around the country. Dates and places are listed on the NAACP's web site.

For more information go to BestDiversityEmployers.com on the World Wide Web.

FAIR SHARE PROGRAM

The Fair Share Program was created in the early 1980s to ensure that a fair share of the dollars spent by African-American consumers are reinvested in black communities in the form of jobs and business opportunities. The Fair Share Program seeks to expand African America's relationship with corporations by

- establishing minority vendor programs for purchasing goods and services
- using aggressive affirmative action programs to create opportunities for advancing African-Americans into senior management positions, including representation on corporate boards
- creating investment and ownership opportunities for African-American businesses
- promoting philanthropic contributions to worthy African-American causes

The Fair Share Program has both a local and a national component. NAACP branches and state conferences focus their efforts on companies with local or regional markets. The national office directs its attention to firms with a national market.

For more information write to
Programs Department
NAACP National Headquarters
4805 Mt. Hope Drive
Baltimore, MD 21215

RELIGIOUS AFFAIRS

The National Congress of Black Churches, as well as individual denominations, provides critical support to the NAACP for the political and economic empowerment of African-

Americans. The major responsibility of the Religious Affairs program is to foster a cooperative relationship between the religious community and the NAACP. The department helps mobilize mass support for voter registration and to defeat legislation contrary to the philosophy of the NAACP.

For more information contact:

Reverend Julius C. Hope, pastor, New Grace Baptist Church, Highland Park, Michigan

(313) 869-3717

VOTER EMPOWERMENT

The voter empowerment program focuses on voter education and registration, and a get-out-the-vote effort. This includes developing voter and issue education programs that heighten awareness about the importance of voting and knowing the positions of candidates for public office with regard to these issues.

Coalitions with other national organizations are developed to maximize collective efforts.

For more information contact:

Programs Department

NAACP National Headquarters

4805 Mt. Hope Drive

Baltimore, MD 21215

**For information on other NAACP programs and divisions
go to www.naacp.org**

CALL FOR
CENTENNIAL SUBMISSIONS

⟫◆⟪

The NAACP will complete its first one hundred years in 2009. To celebrate this significant milestone, we will publish a book to commemorate the NAACP's first century. This will include anecdotes, stories, and poems as well as quotations about the NAACP's impact on American life. Anyone, whether a member of the NAACP or not, who wishes to share an experience that an individual or group has had with the NAACP is welcome to make a submission. To submit material for possible inclusion in this historic publication, please follow the guidelines below.

- **Length** of each submission should not exceed fifteen hundred words.
- If submission has previously been published, be sure to include the name of the publication including author, title, publisher, publication date.
- **Unpublished submissions** are welcomed so long as the author can be verified.

• Include your name, address, telephone number, and/or E-mail address.

E-mail submissions to **blackquotations@earthlink.net**
Subject: **NAACP Centennial**

CONTACT INFORMATION

NAACP
4805 Mt. Hope Drive
Baltimore, MD 21215-3297
(410) 358-8900

Twenty-four-hour public information line
(410) 521-4939

www.naacp.org

NAACP MEMBERSHIP APPLICATION

Please Print

Date: _____

Mr./Mrs./Ms: _____

Street Address: _____

City: _____ State: _____ Zip: _____

Branch Affiliation (if known): _____

Current Membership No. (if renewal): _____

Regular Annual Membership

Regular Adult	$30 [ ]
Youth with Crisis	$15 [ ]
Youth without Crisis	$10 [ ]
Annual Corporate	$5,000 [ ]

Lifetime Membership

Junior Life (date of birth _____)	$100 [ ]
Bronze Life (date of birth _____)	$400 [ ]
Silver Life	$750 [ ]
Gold Life	$1,500 [ ]
Diamond Life	$2,500 [ ]

Method of Payment: Check [ ] Credit Card [ ]

Card Type: _____Card Number: _____

Amount: _____ Expiration: _____

Signature: _____

Make checks payable to the NAACP

Mail to:
Membership Department
National Association for the Advancement of Colored People
4805 Mt. Hope Drive
Baltimore, Maryland 21215

INDEX

H

Haley, Alex (Alexander Palmer), 160

Hall, Edythe Flemings, 122

Hamer, Fannie Lou, 12, 141

Hargrove, Roy, 85

Harrison, Richard Berry, 160

Hastie, William H., 160

Hayes, Roland, 161

Height, Dorothy I., 41, 135, 161

Henry, Aaron, 35, 37, 58, 108, 138

Hickman, Holsey O., 60

Higginbotham, A. Leon, 146, 161

Hill, Lauryn, 51, 79

Hollings, Darius, 43

Hooks, Benjamin L., 7, 88, 142, 153, 154, 161

Hoover, Herbert, 101

Hope, John, 161

Hope, Julius C., 6, 21, 114, 144

Horne, Lena, 104, 161

Houston, Charles Hamilton, 59, 121, 134, 161

Hughes, Langston, 58, 140, 161

Hunt, Henry A., 162

J

Jackson, Jesse, 48, 52, 162

Jackson, Lillie Carroll, 19

Jarrett, Vernon, 4, 90, 153

Johnson, Cora Lee, 57

Johnson, James Weldon, 9, 10, 20, 71, 129, 150, 162

Johnson, Jeffrey, 40

Johnson, John H., 67, 92, 95, 162

Johnson, Lyndon B., 102, 103

Johnson, Magic (Earvin), 46

Johnson, Mordecai Wyatt, 162

Jones, Elaine R., 121

Jones, James Earl, 117

Jones, Quincy, 66

Jones, Robert, 44

Jordan, Barbara, 14, 29, 162

Jordan, Michael, 45, 83

Jordan, Vernon, 114, 162

Julian, Percy L., 162

Just, Ernest E., 163

K-L

Keith, Damon J., 163

Kennedy, Flo, 5

King, Martin Luther, Jr., 45, 62, 99, 110, 163

LaBelle, Patti, 73

Lawless, Theodore K., 163

Lawrence, Jacob, 163

Lee, Spike (Shelton), 90, 111

Lewis, David Levering, 131

Lewis, Reginald, 47

JANET CHEATHAM BELL has taught African-American literature and been an education consultant and textbook editor. Since 1984 she has had a successful writing, speaking, and consulting business. Bell resides in the San Francisco Bay Area and may be contacted via her Web site, www.famousblackquotations.com

(Photo by Kelly Page)

DISCARD

081 TILL

Till victory is won

METRO

R4002009903